Gary McIntosh and Alan Mc[...] [...]rkers in the work of the Lord. I greatly a[...] [...] [...]ave done on this book. Churches in a multi-ethnic community must be multi-ethnic in their ministry. However, not all churches are multi-ethnic, especially those churches that are in a community that represent one socioeconomic class or ethnic group. Therefore, no church should ever be intentionally segregated and remain a New Testament church. This book will help you understand and plan how to fulfill the Great Commission in your community.

—**Elmer L. Towns**, cofounder, Liberty University, Lynchburg, Virginia

McIntosh and McMahan do an outstanding job of highlighting the challenges and opportunities of being the church in today's changing cultural mix. Their insights based on solid research and personal experiences provide a marvelous foundation on which to build effective ministry. If you are looking for a work that will provide a common-sense approach to ministry in our multi-ethnic world, this book needs to be part of your resource tool kit.

—**Phil Stevenson**, director of Church Multiplication & Leadership Development, Pacific-Southwest District, The Wesleyan Church

This volume should be required reading for every pastor in the United States! The authors have done a massive amount of research into the demographic changes that have taken place in this nation in the last ten years, changes that affect every church. Their evaluation of how various churches are dealing or not dealing with the situation is worth the price of the book itself. The comparisons to the New Testament church and their insights from that study reveal a solid biblical basis for all their recommendations. In our ever-changing society, I am proud to highly recommend this very helpful volume.

—**L. David Beckman**, president emeritus, Colorado Christian University

Being the Church in a Multi-Ethnic Community is an excellent primer for the serious church leader seeking to be well-informed on the important issues related to multi-ethnic ministry. I especially appreciate the balanced discussion McIntosh and McMahon present on the Homogeneous Unit Principle. Those who have struggled with the imposed guilt of leading a mono-ethnic church will find their words liberating. The value of this book will rise with time as rising trends in immigration and the migration to cities creates new opportunities for the church to share its transformative message.

—**Jeff Mansell**, district superintendent, Greater Ohio District, The Wesleyan Church

Gary and Alan's latest book is insightful for understanding the diversity of the North American population and the complexity of the church's ministry in our multi-ethnic world. This resource helps judicatory leaders and pastors understand the basics of multi-ethnic ministry and possible strategies that can be used to reach as many people for Christ as possible. This is a must read for leaders who are interested in God's kingdom expanding.

—**Doug Talley**, executive state pastor, Indiana Ministries, Church of God

In the late sixties, missions was "over there." That is no longer true. God has brought missions to America! If you are truly interested in ministering to the multi-ethnic, multicultural reality of twenty-first-century America, then this book is a must read. Study it. Understand it. Practice the principles outlined in the text. You and those to whom you minister will be forever grateful!

—**Gordon E. Penfold**, multi-ethnic pastor and director of
Fresh Start Ministries, Holyoke, Colorado

I'm an immigrant to the US since 1973. I'm wondering, "Where was this book then?" *Being the Church in a Multi-Ethnic Community* is timely, because trans-ethnic fusion continues to grow with a never-ending tide. While businesses and corporations have led the way in mutual under-standing and respect, the church is waking up to an old-new reality best stated by Gary McIntosh and Alan McMahan in the first chapter, aptly titled "Pay Attention! The Immigrants Are Here!" This book is a must read.

—**Samuel R. Chand**, author of *Cracking Your Church's Culture Code*

In a burst of enthusiasm, I jotted two references in the margins within the first five pages: Revelation 7:9 and Ephesians 2:14–18. Both passages reflected for me the great ideal—one new humanity by grace through the cross. McIntosh and McMahan reshaped my too-easy idealism and moved me to a more robust grasp of the challenge the great ideal poses in real life. Happily, this book gives readers a language for understanding the complex-ity of the challenges; it also provides a framework within which to embrace the opportunities posed by the diverse ethnic richness that increasingly surrounds us.

—**Carl C. Green**, pastor, educator, organizational development consultant

Being the Church in a Multi-Ethnic Community provides a solid strategy for concrete actions designed to reach people with the gospel. I am especially impressed with the step-by-step instructions for a transitional church. The authors provide a compelling argument for reaching urban centers where ethnic groups are most likely located. They provide a realistic strategy of transitioning existing churches as one tool among many to be used to reach the new ethnic presence in many urban communities.

—**Franklin R. Dumond**, coauthor of *Legacy Churches*; director of congregational ministries, General Association of General Baptists

Written by two seasoned intercultural specialists, this work provides creative and practical multi-ethnic models for reaching our world. Along with insights on current demographic research, the book's questions at the end of each chapter will stimulate church leaders to navigate the complexities of multi-ethnic ministries, creating a unique map for your specific church in fulfilling God's mission of calling all people to himself.

—**Miles (Skip) Lewis**, director of MA in ministry programs, Lancaster Bible College Graduate School

BEING THE CHURCH IN A MULTI-ETHNIC COMMUNITY

Why It Matters and How It Works

Gary L. McIntosh
Alan McMahan

wesleyan
publishing
house

Indianapolis, Indiana

Copyright © 2012 by Gary L. McIntosh and Alan McMahan
Published by Wesleyan Publishing House
Indianapolis, Indiana 46250
Printed in the United States of America
ISBN: 978-0-89827-490-5

Library of Congress Cataloging-in-Publication Data

McIntosh, Gary, 1947-
  Being the church in a multi-ethnic community : why it matters and how it works / Gary L. McIntosh, Alan McMahan.
      p. cm.
  Includes bibliographical references (p.   ).
  ISBN 978-0-89827-490-5
1. Multiculturalism--Religious aspects--Christianity. 2. Multiculturalism--United States. 3. Church. 4. Church and minorities--United States. 5. Church work with minorities--United States. 6. Ethnicity--Religious aspects--Christianity. 7. Ethnicity--United States. I. McMahan, Alan. II. Title.
  BV639.M56M43 2012
  277.3'083089--dc23
                                        2012001257

To Terri, Billy, and Jonathan who, each in their own way, have been supportive through many hours of labor and provided much inspiration for the journey.

—Alan McMahan

To the hundreds of students who have attended my classes at Talbot School of Theology over the last quarter century. Thanks for teaching me so much about multi-ethnic ministry.

—Gary L. McIntosh

CONTENTS

ACKNOWLEDGEMENTS

We wish to acknowledge the enormous insights provided by those scholars and practitioners who are on the leading edge of multi-ethnic church innovation. Much thanks goes to Jay Pankratz and Art Lucero of Sunrise Church in Rialto, California, who freely gave of their time and resources to let us observe a successful multi-ethnic church that is actively reaching its community. In similar fashion, Ken Korver and Larry Dove at Emmanuel Reformed Church in Paramount, California, inspired us with the tangible expression of the effort required to move beyond an exclusive mono-ethnic congregation to one that is inclusive of the diversity at their doorstep. Appreciation is also offered to First Baptist Church of Flushing, Queens, which, under the leadership of pastor Henry Kwan, skillfully blends congregations from at least three continents to give us a foreshadowing of what it will be like to have the nations assembled around the throne to worship the Lamb. Special thanks goes also to James Cho, who served as a sounding board regarding the intricate dynamics found among multi-generational immigrant believers who are struggling to find identity and belonging in an adopted land. From these and many other insightful men and women from many different churches, we have been able to assemble some of the insights gathered into these pages.

Thanks to our acquisitions editor, Kevin Scott, and his team at Wesleyan Publishing House, for their excellent work on this book. They were more than patient with us as we worked through the editorial process. This finished book is a result of numerous persons working behind the scenes to provide the best possible book for our readers.

1
PAY ATTENTION! THE IMMIGRANTS ARE HERE!

If Walmart is diverse, then your church can be diverse.
—Rev. David Anderson

Have you taken the Walmart test? If not, it might be time to do so. One day this week, drive to the Walmarts within a twenty-mile radius of your church and see who is shopping there. What you find may surprise you. The United States is dramatically more diverse than it was ten years ago, a fact often unnoticed by church leaders and worshipers.

While most of us have carried on with work, family, and various other activities during the last decade, the US has changed. Reports from the recent census show that the United States is "more diverse from the bottom up."[1] Growth in ethnic populations is observable in nearly every state from Minnesota to California, from Idaho to Texas, and from Florida to Montana. For example, ten years ago 12 percent of Minnesota's population was made up of minorities; it has risen to 17 percent today. According to Minnesota State demographer Tom Gillaspy, "80 percent of the state's population growth since 2000 is attributable to minorities."[2] The black population grew 59 percent, Hispanics are up 75 percent, and Asians increased 51 percent during the last decade in Minnesota. In New Mexico, for the first time ever, the number of Hispanics surpassed whites. Non-Hispanic whites represent

40.5 percent of New Mexico's population today, with 46.3 percent being Hispanic, according to recent census data.[3] Those are but two examples; similar findings are shocking researchers and observers throughout the US as more statistics from the census are reported.

Changes in the patterns of ethnicity are part of a larger growth trend that sees the western United States surpassing the Midwest in population. "Will it play in Peoria?" was a common refrain in the 1960s that referenced that area of the country as the mainstream US population. For marketers and politicians, if something was accepted by the midwesterners, they knew it would also be accepted by the mainstream population elsewhere. The Midwest has been the cultural heartland of the United States since the 1850s (before then it was in West Virginia). Over the last decade, the center of US population has shifted from around Peoria, Illinois, to somewhere in Texas County, Missouri. Peoria, Arizona (a suburb of Phoenix) is now larger than Peoria, Illinois. "Will it play in Peoria?" now makes more sense with reference to Arizona than Illinois.

Where is the fastest growth occurring in the United States? It is in the mountain states of Arizona, Colorado, Montana, Idaho, Wyoming, Utah, Nevada, and New Mexico. Such population growth is primarily driven by the arrival of Latino immigrants who desire what every ethnic population has ever desired—jobs, affordable housing, safety, and opportunity.

AN OLD TREND

The imminent wave of new immigrants coming to America was heralded by *TIME* magazine the week of July 8, 1985, in its cover story, "Immigrants: The Changing Face of America." At the time, the special issue was the largest in *TIME*'s history with over eighty editorial pages. Information was gathered from *TIME*'s ten bureaus, dozens of editors, and scores of writers and correspondents throughout the United States. It was only the fourth time in the history of the magazine that an issue was devoted to one subject. The subject matter covered everything: "education, culture, food, business, religion, indeed every aspect of our lives."[4]

Stories of people from India, Romania, Kampuchea, Afghanistan, Philippines, Ethiopia, Laos, Soviet Union, Ghana, Ireland, Cuba, and South Korea were chronicled.

As the 1985 issue of *TIME* focused on the delights and opportunities created by new immigrants, the challenge of ethnic and cultural change led *TIME* to publish another special issue just eight years later in the fall of 1993. The magazine bore the lead title "The New Face of America: How Immigrants Are Shaping the World's First Multicultural Society." To illustrate the new face of America, particularly the impact of intermarriage, *TIME*'s managing editor commissioned the composition of a computer image by morphing together the photographs of seven men and seven women of different ethnic backgrounds. After sixty-five hours of computer work using a complicated formula, the picture of a woman was created that was reportedly 15 percent Anglo-Saxon, 17.5 percent Middle Eastern, 17.5 percent African, 7.5 percent Asian, 35 percent Southern European, and 7.5 percent Hispanic. The picture was used on the magazine's cover.[5]

However, uniting ethnic peoples into a unified whole proved to be easier on a computer than in real life. In the 1993 issue, *TIME*'s published articles focused on the public's growing resistance to immigration ("Not Quite So Welcome Anymore"), the rise of illegal aliens ("The Shadow of the Law"), the impact of immigrants on the arts ("The Art of Diversity"), the challenge of legal justice in a multi-ethnic society ("Whose Peers?"), and the growing conflict of different religions ("One Nation Under Gods").

Without doubt, the face of the United States has changed and is continuing to change. The new ethnic marketplace is forcing government, business, and churches to rethink how to speak the language and adopt the culture of the new multi-ethnic and multicultural reality.

CHURCHES BEGIN TO RESPOND

While *TIME* was busy documenting the joys and juggernauts of the new ethnic reality in the larger US culture, observers of the church world also alerted church leaders to the new challenges that were coming.

Christianity Today's lead article for July 19, 1985, read "The Overseas Challenge Comes Home: Where are the missionaries to meet the arriving millions?" The article noted that, while there had been different waves of immigration into the United States since the 1800s, the floodgates of new immigrants were opened wide in the 1980s. Mission was coming home to America, but church leaders and people were not ready to receive them or reach them with the gospel. Some leaders, like the late Ralph Winter, saw the future opportunity for mission. He commented, "In the next five years, we are going to witness this century's greatest single mutation in the structure of missions. As a result, missions will no longer be viewed as something we simply do overseas, but something we do within groups of unreached peoples, whether those groups are located in Singapore or Los Angeles."[6] Unfortunately, even though mission leaders like Winter called for churches in the United States to respond, most refused to see the opportunities for mission that the new immigrants brought with them.

Some churches, however, did take notice and began to shift ministry budgets, personnel, and priorities to reach the new ethnic peoples. Just one year following the article in *Christianity Today*, *MissionsUSA*, a publication of the Home Mission Board of the Southern Baptist Convention, published "The American Mosaic: Our Nation of Immigrants." The article reported that each Sunday, Southern Baptists worshiped in eighty-seven languages and dialects. At the time, Southern Baptists reportedly were the most integrated denomination in America with some forty-six hundred congregations representing eighty-four of the nation's five hundred ethnic groups and ninety-seven of the 495 Native American tribes. Since 1974 an average of three new ethnic groups had become part of the Southern Baptist Convention.[7]

A GROWING INTEREST

If only a few churches and denominations grasped the enormous realities and consequences of the new immigrants coming to the United States in the 1980s, today it appears many have a growing concern. Interest in starting new churches to reach different ethnic groups is seen from all corners, including The Wesleyan Church, Church of God Anderson, Baptist General Conference, the Evangelical Free Church, the Foursquare Church, the Assemblies of God, and Southern Baptists. Church planting is viewed as the main and best way to win new peoples to Christ. But another major emphasis is gaining interest: planting multi-ethnic churches.

Since the 1960s, when people pointed out that Sunday morning was the most segregated hour in the United States, church leaders have longed for the day when those of different ethnic backgrounds would worship together in local congregations. That dream is finally being realized from coast to coast. Today, multi-ethnic churches are readily found in New York City, Chicago, and Los Angeles, as well as in Little Rock, Portland, and Phoenix.

A decade ago, Grace Chapel in Lexington, Massachusetts (a suburb of Boston) was nearly 100 percent white. Today, it is estimated that 25 percent of worshipers are minorities, with three groups—Koreans, Haitians, and Chinese—being the main ones. The church has even called a pastor of multicultural ministries to help steer the church's outreach toward ethnic peoples in the larger community. Grace Chapel is just one example among numerous large churches that are seeking to become more ethnically diverse.

Smaller churches are also interested in becoming a church representative of all nations. Open Table Community Church in Chamblee, Georgia, is one example. Five years ago, the church's worship attendees were 99 percent white. After the pastor caught a new vision for a multi-ethnic church, the church relocated three times to get closer to immigrant and refugee communities in order to reach them for Christ, as well as to learn from them. Today the church's main board is 50 percent nonwhite, and 30 percent of the congregation is made up of diverse ethnic peoples. Similar churches are springing up all over the United States, from Compton, California, to Dayton, Ohio, and from Grand Rapids, Michigan, to Seattle, Washington.

But while the dream of multi-ethnic churches is slowly becoming a reality in the US, there are a growing array of models and little understanding of the characteristics, patterns, and problems of such churches among church leaders. Anyone who has tried to start a multi-ethnic church or turn an older church into a multi-ethnic community of faith realizes there are enormous challenges, misunderstandings, and difficulties to overcome in the process to become increasingly diverse.

WHY THIS BOOK?

While North American church leaders know a great deal about planting and growing mono-ethnic churches, most struggle with reaching new ethnic groups and establishing multi-ethnic churches. Thus, we have written *Being the Church in a Multi-Ethnic Community: Why It Matters and How It Works* to serve as an introductory guide, a basic primer to provide an overview of the issues, challenges, and essential principles to develop multi-ethnic churches in the United States.

A small sampling of the questions you will find answered in this book include . . .

- What is a multi-ethnic church?
- Can a multi-ethnic church truly be multicultural?
- Why are multi-ethnic churches important in the United States?
- What is fueling the interest in multi-ethnic churches today?
- How is the Homogeneous Unit Principle to be understood in a multi-ethnic context?
- What are the major multi-ethnic models being used in the United States?
- What are the common denominators, patterns, or practices being used among multi-ethnic churches?
- What are the major barriers or challenges in designing multi-ethnic churches?
- Must all churches be multi-ethnic?
- What are the best options and approaches to use in starting multi-ethnic churches in the United States?

Most books available today address the multi-ethnic church from narrow perspectives. Some tell the story of only one church, others focus on specific ethnic groups, and still others stress one model or viewpoint of multi-ethnic ministry. While such books provide important information, *Being the Church in a Multi-Ethnic Community* seeks to cover the basic missiological issues involved. We define *missiology* simply as "the study of how peoples come to God in history."[8] By peoples we mean the various individuals, families, clans, tribes, and ethnic groups in the world, or what the Bible calls "the nations" (*ta ethne* of Matt. 28:19–20). By "come to God in history", we mean an analysis and synthesis of the theological, sociological, anthropological, historical, and practical processes that God uses to bring all peoples to himself. Hence, this book is not just an analysis of individual parts of multi-ethnic ministry but an exploration of the dynamic synthesis of all the parts. Ministry always takes place in context, and this book attempts to alert the reader to many of the ingredients that form the North American context for multi-ethnic ministry. Each chapter analyzes a specific aspect of missiology, while synthesis comes together gradually throughout the book.

Missiology in North America is dynamic, not static. It responds to new challenges, fresh contexts, and emerging models. No living person can adequately engage the complex, interacting pulses that make up missiology in North America, let alone the world. However, we hope to introduce you, the reader, to the interplay of missiological theory, field research, and biblical mission. Part of the challenge is separating the eternal from the changing, while allowing for both to exist in dynamic tension. We serve an eternal God and communicate an eternal gospel. But we serve and communicate such to real people in time and culture. It is our desire that *Being the Church in a Multi-Ethnic Community* will aid you to be faithful in winning all peoples to personal faith in Jesus Christ, and to bring them into Christ's church where they can serve him as their Lord and Savior. "That is [the] goal, that the Great Commission of Jesus to His Church may continue in our day and generation, and the Gospel may be heard, the lives of people transformed, and they may be incorporated into His Church, and have fellowship with Him and with each other."[9]

An important aspect of this book is that both of us are missiologists, having experience both in the United States and in other countries. Together we bring over sixty years of ministry experience—cross-cultural and mono-cultural—to the discussion of this important aspect of ministry.

Alan has served as a vice president for the Alliance Theological Seminary in Nyack, New York, and as the academic dean at The King's College in midtown Manhattan. He currently is associate professor of intercultural studies at Biola University. A former missionary in Indonesia, Alan has worked with churches in North America and on the Pacific Rim and has taught in the areas of missiology, church growth, leadership, organizational development, and evangelism. He is active in training undergraduate and graduate students including mid-career professionals, schoolteachers, pastors, and denominational leaders throughout the United States, Canada, and much of Southeast Asia in the effective means to develop leaders and grow churches. He holds a PhD from Fuller Theological Seminary and a ThM from Asbury Theological Seminary in missiology, as well as an MDiv in missions from Alliance Theological Seminary. He is listed in *Who's Who Among America's Teachers* and has received the Leadership Award and the Donald McGavran Church Growth Award from Fuller Theological Seminary. He is general editor of the *Great Commission Research Journal.*

Gary is a nationally and internationally known author, speaker, consultant, and professor of Christian ministry and leadership at Talbot School of Theology, also of Biola University. He has written extensively in the field of pastoral ministry, leadership, generational studies, and church growth. He received his BA from Colorado Christian University in biblical studies, an MDiv from Western Seminary in pastoral studies, a DMin from Fuller Theological Seminary in church growth studies, and a PhD in intercultural studies also from Fuller Theological Seminary. Gary has served over twelve hundred churches in more than eighty denominations throughout the United States and Canada, and he edits the popular *Growth Points* newsletter.

GETTING STARTED

If this is the first time you have considered the multi-ethnic church challenge, it is best to start with chapter 2 and read through all chapters as written. Attacking the issue with this approach provides a step-by-step, logical progression to the issues. On the other hand, if you have read other books or are familiar with the challenges of designing a multi-ethnic church, read over the table of contents and start with the chapter that attracts your attention and interest. While each chapter builds on the one before, each is generally written so that it can stand alone. You will find that some information is repeated throughout this book. We intentionally did this so that those readers who do not read the chapters in order will still have important information.

You will notice right away that we seek to stay in the middle of the road. We are not unabashed multi-ethnic church proponents, but we do believe churches must move toward greater inclusiveness and cultural sensitivity in our day. But we also believe that mono-ethnic churches are biblical and needed too. From our perspective, it will take all kinds of churches—mono-ethnic and multi-ethnic—to reach all the nations for Christ.

Demographers predict the population of the United States will top four hundred million by the middle of the twenty-first century.[10] Most of these people will live in urban centers of the United States, which will place at least 90 percent or more of Americans in close proximity with people of other ethnicities and cultures. In fact, this is already happening. For example, in a suburb of Seattle, Washington, a study of the people occupying ten randomly selected homes found the following different families: one family each from India, Singapore, Mexico, Samoa, Ethiopia, Russia, and—from the United States—two Caucasians, one Native American, and one African-American. All of these families lived on the same block! In such situations, which are going to be more prominent in the future, multi-ethnic churches are likely to be present. Now is the time to prepare for future realities. *Being the Church in a Multi-Ethnic Community* will help you get ready.

PUTTING INSIGHTS TO WORK

1. Do you see ethnic changes in your community? If so, describe what you see. Are new businesses being established? Are new languages being used? Describe as specifically as possible what you observe.

2. In what ways is ethnic change impacting your church and its ministry? Describe the impact on outreach, welcoming of newcomers, growth and decline in attendance, experience in worship, and other areas.

3. How is your church responding to the ethnic changes in your area? In what ways is your ministry adapting or changing? What must change in the future?

2
DEFINING THE MULTI-ETHNIC CHURCH

*The complexity of society means the complexity of the church.
We need to realize that we live in a multi-ethnic world.*
—Alan Tippett

What sounds like a simple task at first often turns out to be much more difficult in practice. Such is the situation when attempting to define a multi-ethnic church. That the study of this topic is still in its infancy is evidenced by the fact that many people use a wide variety of terms to describe roughly the same phenomenon. In a survey of the current literature one encounters terms such as *multinational*, *multiracial*, *multi-ethnic*, and *multicultural* to describe churches where the people come from diverse backgrounds. However, further inspection reveals that these terms are not all equal in meaning, with each term revealing various shades of complexity.

To aid us in thinking through possible definitions, it is helpful to think of words as either less or more precise, less or more complex (see figure 2.1). For example, as one moves from the left to the right in the figure, the terms become more specific and complex. *Multiracial* is the most confusing term. It has roots in the study of genetics, ancestral populations, and medicine. Technically, the word *race* is not a biblical term, and when different versions of the Bible occasionally use the word, it refers to a family, nation, or generation of mankind. Even secular writers and researchers now understand the concept of race to be nothing more than a social construction.[1] Unfortunately, we are not likely to see the word disappear anytime soon, since it has found a place in the literature of society. Though different cultures classify people differently, scientists generally group all of humanity into forty-two native population groups that form nine population clusters.[2] The term *multiracial* is less useful for church ministry today since it tends to carry negative emotional baggage.

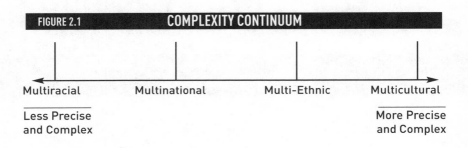

FIGURE 2.1   **COMPLEXITY CONTINUUM**

Multiracial   Multinational   Multi-Ethnic   Multicultural

Less Precise   More Precise
and Complex   and Complex

The second term, *multinational*, is also of little help for talking about a diverse church. There are approximately 195 nations in the world; this number is frequently changing and subject to political opinion.[3] Mission agencies used to think in terms of sending workers "to the nations" before greater precision emerged at the first Lausanne Congress on World Evangelism in 1974. At that conference, missiologist Ralph Winter changed the course of mission thinking by introducing a concept called "unreached peoples."[4] Since that time, the strategy has shifted to establishing a church in every ethnic group or people group in the world, while introducing a more precise term: *multi-ethnic*.

Multi-ethnic reflects most accurately the biblical concept of "the peoples," and we feel it is the most helpful term when speaking about churches that are comprised of different families, clans, or cultural groups. When Ralph Winter catalyzed the concept of "unreached peoples," he simply reiterated the Great Commission of Christ to reach every family, tribe, and ethnic group (*ta ethne*) in the world. Genesis 11 lists about seventy groups. Today, missiologists calculate the world's population to be roughly composed of 17,500 distinct ethnic groups.[5] These groups are defined by having a distinct language and culture into which the gospel needs to be proclaimed. Ethnicity is also often a bigger determiner of a people's identity and world-view than race or nationality. Consider the fact that there may be many ethnicities that compose a single nationality, each with its own unique point of view. For practical reasons, we often group people together in cultural families rather than separate them out, identifying them as "Latinos," "Asians," "Anglos," or "African-Americans."[6] Yet, in doing so, we run the risk of ignoring the differences and glossing over the complexities between them.

For example, Alan consulted in a large black church in Brooklyn a few years back. To the uninformed person, this black church might be seen as a typical, successful African-American church. Further inspection, however, reveals significant differences. For one, the church does not draw its members primarily from a predominantly African-American neighborhood. Rather the members of this church converge together each Sunday from a wide geographical area, sometimes traveling ninety minutes or more from where they live. Nor do the members of the church understand or identify with the history of racial discrimination that has been a part of the experience of the majority of the local population. This church is distinctly optimistic toward the future and in the cultural style it employs. As immigrants from throughout the Caribbean, they think of themselves as different from African-Americans that harbor memories of the 1950s civil rights movement in the United States. They are very eager to pursue higher education, economic security, and success. They reject being labeled as victims or dispossessed. They aspire to make a name for themselves and their children. Interestingly, they cluster together in a cultural family group with a relatively common identity as being Caribbean and Central American immigrants, even though they really came from perhaps a dozen countries and represent numerous ethnicities. *Multi-ethnic* is a good term to use in describing this church and most others in today's diverse environment.

Multicultural, another widely used term, is the most complex of the terms that can be used in describing heterogeneous churches; but it is not always positive. Not only is the term associated negatively with multiculturalism, which carries connotations of postmodern universalism,[7] but it also invites other misunderstandings and complexities. For example, most multi-ethnic churches cannot nuance or contextualize their ministries sufficiently to really function on a full multicultural level. While they may be composed of people from a wide variety of ethnic backgrounds, they most often operate under the rules of a dominant cultural group. More will be discussed on this later, but it is enough to note at the moment that there may be significant cultural variations even among members of a single ethnicity. To recognize the various worldviews and cultural rule sets that govern these diverse peoples is difficult. For example, what many call a Latino church may, in truth, hide the fact that under this label may exist people from Guatemala, Cuba, Mexico, Honduras, Panama, Puerto Rico, or even South America or Spain, each with their own unique culture, worldview, and preferred worship style.

To really operate a church that gives room for unique expressions of each of these groups is beyond the capacity of most congregations. As a means of managing the overwhelming complexity of cultural variations, most congregations, even if they aspire to be culturally sensitive, simply give a nod to the cultural variations of their members. Grouping people around a common language reduces complexity and cultural fatigue, but doing so usually glosses over significant differences between them. Ultimately, most multicultural churches develop a monocultural pattern of life, in which each distinct ethnic group blends into some common denominator, essentially making the church monocultural.

Of the four possible terms (there may be more in the future) we prefer *multi-ethnic*. From a missiological perspective, this word fits both the biblical concept and current understanding the best. What then is a good definition of a multi-ethnic church? Some have suggested that it must have certain intentions. For example, Ken Davis defines a multi-ethnic church as "a biblical community of believers who (1) intentionally recruit, recognize, and embrace a diversity of peoples; (2) are committed to racial reconciliation;

and (3) are working out administrative structures that assure the continuation of both unity and diversity."[8] This description is a noble aspiration and is helpful as a statement of intention. But it unnecessarily narrows the definition of a multi-ethnic church compared to what we observe in the field. One study concluded that 96 percent of the churches in North America, which are not in the middle of an ethnic transition, have 80 percent of their congregation representing only one ethnic group.[9] That leaves only 4 percent that would fit Davis's narrow definition of multi-ethnic.

Some sociologists have defined a multi-ethnic church based on a numerical threshold. Mark DeYmaz notes that sociologists with whom he consults use the rule that if no single ethnic group composes more than 80 percent of the total congregation, that congregation is to be considered multi-ethnic.[10] If one goes by head-count totals alone, this criterion may serve as a good definition. At least it allows us to speak with greater precision than we might have done otherwise.

Our research leads us to believe that both of these definitions are inadequate. When we define a multi-ethnic church too narrowly, we unintentionally exclude churches that are, in some fashion, multi-ethnic, but perhaps not intentionally operating according to the ideals described in either definition above.

A better definition is offered by the late missiologist Paul Hiebert, who says, a multi-ethnic church is "a church in which there is (1) an attitude and practice of accepting people of all ethnic, class and national origins as equal and fully participating members and ministers in the fellowship of the church; and (2) the manifestation of this attitude and practice by the involvement of people from different ethnic, social and national communities as members in the church."[11] This definition does not establish a percentage criteria nor does it establish any particular model or format that must characterize a multi-ethnic church. We feel this is a healthier and more realistic definition, since the reality is that multi-ethnic churches come in all shapes, sizes, and makeups. There is a range of possibilities where a church can honestly be considered multi-ethnic. The following descriptions help clarify some of the possibilities.

THE ABC'S OF ETHNICITY

Dirke Johnson describes the ABCs of ethnicity that were created for the dominant culture to understand where on the cultural spectrum a minority person might be at any given point in time.[12]

FIGURE 2.2   ETHNICITY CONTINUUM[13]

Assimilated ⟵⟶ Bicultural ⟵⟶ Contextualized

In this model, persons of a minority culture, and even entire groups, are viewed as being at one of three possible points: (A) assimilated into the dominant culture, in effect leaving behind his or her roots; (B) in the bicultural middle ground able to navigate two cultures, his or her own minority culture group as well as the dominant culture; or (C) remaining solidly contextualized within his or her own cultural group and essentially disengaged from the majority culture.

Looking across the ecclesiastical spectrum, one can find multi-ethnic churches that fit each one of these three patterns. Some multi-ethnic churches have a number of ethnic peoples that operate together according to the cultural rule set of the dominant cultural group (pattern A above). Such a pattern is especially present among some second-generation immigrants who have been assimilated into the dominant culture in the public school system and seek churches that offer a worship style aligned with the dominant culture. Third-generation ethnics are also often found at point A, having fully assimilated into the host culture. A second type of church is composed of autonomous or semi-autonomous groups in which people rarely interact with each other. They remain loosely held together, functioning often in different foreign-language worship services and small groups (pattern C above). A third type of multi-ethnic church is more truly bicultural and seeks to blend the cultural patterns of the ethnicities represented in terms of worship styles, discipleship models, leadership forms, and governance patterns (pattern B above). This type of church almost always is comprised of second-generation ethnics who feel comfortable navigating two different cultures. Any one of these three types can be multi-ethnic if they accept and empower different people groups in some manner. However, there are additional aspects of cultural interaction that make the possible models even more complex.

Sociologists have noted that interacting ethnic groups have centripetal or centrifugal tendencies.[14] When a group acts centripetally toward other groups, it pulls inward toward itself and is more likely to accept common values and lifestyles and participate in common groups and associations. That is to say, it is more likely to seek heterogeneous groups where a wide variety of people seek unity around a common issue or value. For some churches the value might be promoting racial reconciliation in an area torn by racial division. For other churches it might be a common cultural denominator, which was true with the multinational, Caribbean immigrant church Alan consulted. Even though that congregation was comprised of people from multiple cultures and indigenous languages, they nevertheless found more in common with other ethnicities from their region than they did with people from another cultural block, like Asians or Anglos. Other churches may gather around a life stage or career path. A good example of this is Redeemer Presbyterian Church in New York City, which is diverse in ethnicity but homogeneous in age, marital status, and education. The congregation is composed of people in their twenties and thirties who are highly educated, single, and upwardly mobile.

When an ethnic group acts centrifugally toward other groups, it is more likely to gravitate out, away from itself and toward its distinct homogeneous clusters where it works to preserve its distinctiveness, whether that be in the area of religion, language, or recreational pursuits. Certainly even multi-generational churches (which describes most churches) tend to separate by age and common interests. In a multi-ethnic context, there are even more reasons than mere age categories that propel people into clusters with others similar to themselves.

To understand the potential multi-ethnic models, Elizabeth Drury proposed some helpful metaphors for assessing differently structured multi-ethnic congregations.[15] Some multi-ethnic churches, she argues, function like "mall churches," where each homogeneous congregation opens up its own unique storefront in a shared facility. Some multi-ethnic churches function as "cinema churches," where diverse peoples meet in the same room and watch the same movie with the help of subtitles. Then there are blended models that contain both heterogeneous and homogeneous groups where both types of structures coexist in the same congregation. For example, a church may have a common, multi-ethnic worship service but also language-specific worship services, discipleship classes, or small groups.

VARIETIES OF MULTI-ETHNIC CHURCH MODELS

To further expand on how multiple congregations associate with each other, share resources, and join together on ministry initiatives, Drury offers the following metaphors. Multiple congregations associate with one another:

- as isolated renters, like separate vendors at a flea market;
- as like-minded but impersonal investors, like partners in a salon;
- as occasionally hospitable neighbors, who feel good about one another and the neighborhood but who pursue separate goals;
- as cooperative coworkers, who collaborate on joint projects but keep a safe interpersonal distance and protect resources; and
- as loving siblings, committed to a family relationship through thick and thin, around the dinner table.[16]

Drury then goes on to illustrate what churches in each of these types would look like in practice as they progress toward greater levels of mutuality and interdependence.

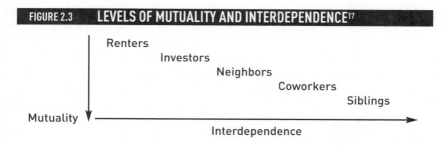

FIGURE 2.3   LEVELS OF MUTUALITY AND INTERDEPENDENCE[17]

Renter churches may take the form of a declining Caucasian church that now has a membership of a couple dozen people that supports its budget by renting its facilities out to minority church groups that may or may not line up with its own doctrinal positions. As long as the rent is paid, the arrangement works with no interaction between the congregations.

Investor churches sometimes occur when a Hispanic congregation, for example, desires to rent facilities from a large Anglo congregation that is a part of the same denomination. These congregations do not necessarily interact with each other, but they subscribe to the same doctrinal standards and perhaps show affiliation to the same denomination through signage or shared advertising. As long as the guest church helps maintain the property and honor the usage schedule for the facilities, everyone is happy.

Neighborhood churches are churches that intend to be more collaborative in selected areas of common interest. In multi-ethnic areas these churches may attempt to show greater acceptance to the diversity of peoples around them without necessarily changing how they fundamentally serve their own people. For most of their ministry functions, they stay within their own homogeneous congregations (more about homogeneity in chapter 8). The Anglo congregation, the Hispanic congregation, and the Hmong congregation, for example, have their own pastors, discipleship groups, and worship services; but they agree in their doctrinal statements, share expenses, and occasionally sponsor joint fellowship activities that draw the diverse congregations together. Drury points out, however, that the bond shared by such congregations may not be strong enough to survive conflict if it emerges.

Coworker churches are even more deliberate in combining efforts for special outreach events or holiday activities. Tribal leaders of the various congregations collaborate with the other chiefs and then go back to their people with the orders for the next joint activity. Efforts are made to honor the other groups and make sure each group does an equal share of the work, while avoiding embarrassment.

Many multi-ethnic churches, perhaps most, aspire to be like Drury's fifth type, the sibling church. This model assumes the multi-ethnic church is able to create a level playing field in which each ethnic group takes an equal amount of responsibility and privilege from the joint interaction. In this world, no one group dominates, and the context is one of mutual trust, sharing, collaboration, and fellowship. It is a church where ethnic hostility is broken down, and there is no distinction made between people on the basis of ethnicity, language, culture, gender, or financial capacity. It is the church that is characterized by reconciliation and harmony. It is heaven on earth.[18]

The sibling church is difficult to achieve. So pernicious is human nature that it is rare to find a church that is truly color-blind, impartial, and fair. Despite our best efforts, we instinctively judge people on the basis of external appearance, personal prosperity, and social eloquence. The history of ethnic relations in the area, the skills of the leadership, and the level of commitment of the various constituencies all play a part to determine whether this experiment is successful. We are being honest in this evaluation. It is certainly worth the effort to try developing a sibling church. We should make the attempt while understanding the nature of the challenge.

If the sibling church is difficult to achieve, it is even more difficult to maintain over time. In any multi-ethnic church, it is very unlikely that all ethnic constituencies are the same size and equally influential. Furthermore, as one group loses members because of demographic shifts in the community or gets larger through successful outreach, it is natural that it will have more or fewer leaders and an increasing or declining voice. As a result, many sibling churches are inherently unstable structures. While they aspire to the highest ideals of mutual respect and egalitarian cooperation, they are difficult to manage and maintain.

What Elizabeth Drury's metaphors do for us is show the great variety of multi-ethnic church models and variations that are possible. At what point of mutuality and interdependence (see figure 2.3) does a church become truly multi-ethnic? How much intentionality and collaboration is required before a church meets the definition? At minimum, Drury's metaphors prompt us to be more precise in how we define the multi-ethnic church.

Another way to look at this question is by thinking of levels or degrees of multi-ethnic blending. As the metaphors above indicate, some churches are multi-ethnic only because they share the same building. They really do not blend their congregations. Some churches are only occasionally multi-ethnic when they come together on special occasions for a potluck or holiday service. Some churches are multi-ethnic only in certain ministry functions, such as outreach or worship.

Closer inspection of some self-proclaimed multi-ethnic churches reveals that they are primarily multi-ethnic in their worship attendance. That is, the worshiping congregants represent a wide diversity of ethnicities. However, the culture of the service is decidedly monocultural. Dirke Johnson points out "most churches called multicultural are monocultural churches (usually White-cultured) with a multiracial membership."[19] Redeemer Presbyterian Church in New York City has a large number of Asian attendees but employs a classical worship style in the morning services and a jazz worship style in the evenings. There is not even a nod to any type of Asian culture.

Some churches desire to be much more intentional in welcoming and celebrating the diversity that is in the congregation. Emmanuel Reformed Church in Paramount, California, is a diverse congregation composed of the descendants of white, Dutch dairy farmers, African-Americans, and more recently arrived Latino families. A multi-ethnic team of musicians and worship leaders leads the church's worship service that includes a gospel music choir with Latino highlights. They have gone a step further by intentionally weaving various cultural traditions into a single service. However, they still have a separate Spanish language service and a more traditional-oriented (Anglo-oriented) service earlier in the day on Sunday. Their most musically diverse service is the 12:15 p.m. service on Sunday.

Other churches are multi-ethnic in larger venues. Associate pastor Art Lucero of Sunrise Church in Rialto, California, discovered a good example of this pattern. Through a carefully designed sociological study in this highly multi-ethnic church, Lucero sampled the congregation to see if members developed friends with people of other ethnicities in their closest friendship circles.[20] What he discovered surprised the entire staff. Their members' circle of closest friends is surprisingly homogeneous. Almost all of the members' closest friends are of the same ethnic and cultural background. Even after decades of intentional effort to build an ethnically heterogeneous church, Sunrise Church is still largely composed of small homogeneous units at the closest friendship level.

Perhaps the most difficult level of multi-ethnicity to achieve is in the upper leadership circles. Most intentional multi-ethnic churches have pastors and lay leaders that mirror the ethnic diversity of the congregation. However, creating a leadership structure that mirrors all the decision-making and leadership styles of the various ethnicities is a level of complexity that few master. Even if the worship styles, disciple-making structures, and outreach efforts capture the brilliance and creativity of the various contributing cultures, making decisions in a way that honors the cultural traditions of each ethnic constituency is daunting. Too often governing boards resort to Roberts Rules of Order or some other democratically fashioned system without considering that their very way of making decisions comes out of a set of values that are culturally informed.

Asian cultures, for example, usually value indirect leadership styles, often defer to the oldest among them, are more hierarchical in nature, and function to preserve tradition. This style may be offensive to certain Western approaches that are more direct, egalitarian, and value youth and innovation.

Quoting Charles Gilmore, president of the Impact Movement, Dirke Johnson makes the point that multi-ethnic church leadership structures often do not take each ethnic group's decision-making processes seriously: "'Do White Christians respect the leadership of Black Christian leaders and their spiritual tradition, and that of cultures other than their own?' All too often Black church leaders are not brought to the table as equals, but rather as endorsers or tokens. They are expected to go along with the already determined agenda. Rather than setting the agenda, they are usually expected to give credence to it with their respective constituencies."[21]

Clearly, blending leadership styles from multiple ethnicities can be difficult. If a church is to go beyond tokenism, there must be a serious attempt to honor the leadership styles of contributing groups. Yet this can lead to conflict and even gridlock if uncertainty is created on how decisions get made.

To put this model together in a more graphical way, the following diagram is offered.

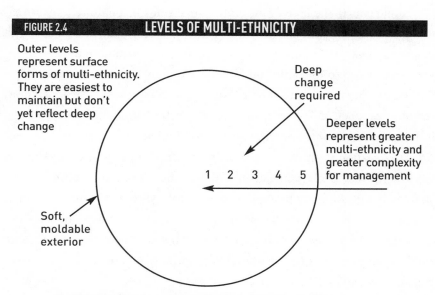

FIGURE 2.4   LEVELS OF MULTI-ETHNICITY

Outer levels represent surface forms of multi-ethnicity. They are easiest to maintain but don't yet reflect deep change

Deep change required

Deeper levels represent greater multi-ethnicity and greater complexity for management

1   2   3   4   5

Soft, moldable exterior

5. Multiple ethnic congregations sharing the building (renters, investors)
4. Occasionally multi-ethnic (neighbors, coworkers)
3. Multiple ethnicities regularly attending the same service (majority group designed)
2. Worship style celebrates multiple cultures (siblings)
1. Leadership reflects multiple ethnicities (not just leadership composition but decision-making styles)

A good multi-ethnic model recognizes that apparent culture change can happen on the surface without affecting the deep-seated values and ethos of a people. External change is highly visible and can be made rapidly and often without a lot of effort. Just like an overripe Georgia peach can be easily indented with the slight pressure of the finger, it does not usually take much effort to make a change on the surface. Such change is deceptive, leading the change agent to deduce that the observable gives evidence of the deep-seated changes he or she desires. But like a peach, surface-level changes may hide what actually is true underneath. Indeed many multi-ethnic churches that pride themselves on the breadth of their diversity and open-mindedness may actually be driven by the dominant ethnic group with only a nod toward the multiple cultures that make up the congregation.

As one cuts to the core of the culture, one finds that culture transformation is dramatically more difficult to achieve. Every peach has a stony pit that resists change. For all cultures, the deep-seated assumptions and world-view values are so invisible and familiar that they are taken for granted as the "way we do things here" or the "way the world operates." That pit almost seems to be made of Teflon, easily shedding efforts to challenge and change it. Because worldview assumptions are so implicit, it usually takes an outsider to question it. In the School of Intercultural Studies at Biola University where Alan teaches, he tells his students that it is usually easier if they start studying culture by first going to a radically different culture than their own. It is in those contexts that we most easily see the assumptions and ways of thinking that the natives take for granted. It actually requires much more skill to analyze one's own cultural assumptions. As commonly acknowledged, "It wasn't a fish that discovered water!"

In a similar fashion, the deeper issues of being a truly multi-ethnic church in which each culture finds expression and value and no one group is dominant generates a level of complexity that only the most cross-culturally astute (and humble) can master. For that reason, the multi-ethnic church that is multicultural on the deepest levels may, in fact, be rare. It may function as an ideal type to provide a goal to move toward, but it is only acquired with great effort and perhaps only for limited periods of time.

It should be clear by now that defining a multi-ethnic church is much more difficult than first imagined. Several factors come together to create different forms and types of multi-ethnic communities of faith. The level of mutuality and interdependence, whether a church is centrifugal or centripetal, and the degree that people are primarily Assimilated, Bicultural, or Contextualized (ABCs) all play a part in the discussion. In the final analysis, some churches that claim to be multi-ethnic are less so than they imagine. Yet, other churches are far more multi-ethnic than they realize.

PUTTING INSIGHTS TO WORK

1. Which of the four terms do you prefer: *multiracial*, *multinational*, *multi-ethnic*, or *multicultural*? Are you familiar with other terms that might be used in this discussion? If so, what are they?

2. Thinking back to Drury's five metaphors of multi-ethnic churches, which one is your church closest to modeling? Why do you select that one?

3. What definition of a multi-ethnic church do you find most helpful in your thinking? How much ethnic blending do you think a church must have to honestly be considered a multi-ethnic church? Why?

THE MULTI-ETHNIC CHURCH IN SCRIPTURE

God's plan of ethnic diversity is at least as old as the earth's first inhabitants.
—Randy Woodley

Dan left the meeting perplexed and irritated. As one of the few pastors in his conference who was leading a growing church, he was proud of the way his church had been effective in reaching out to the community. Already this month several new believers had been added to the family of faith and former attendees were coming back to the church.

In the same fashion as in past years, the district superintendent had brought in a speaker to challenge the status quo and suggest better ways to do ministry. At least that was the intent.

What irritated Dan on this day, however, was the insistence from the guest speaker that a church must be multi-ethnic to be biblical. The speaker's urban church was ethnically diverse with fifteen nationalities represented and modeled reconciliation and unity. The speaker's exposition of Scripture pointed out that God's intention was to reach all nations with the gospel. Dan did not disagree with that premise, as his church was engaged in sending, supporting, and praying for missionaries serving cross-culturally around the world. But for the speaker to lay a guilt-trip on those in the audience for leading mono-ethnic churches made Dan more than a little upset.

The conference did raise a lot of questions: Was it true that his church and all others like it were missing the mark? Were mono-ethnic churches somehow inferior or more self-centered than multi-ethnic churches? Worse yet, were churches like his disobedient to God's will? Dan left the conference seeking more understanding regarding what Scripture has to say about this so he would know what to do next.

Dan's story represents conversations we have engaged in with pastors in the last few years. All too often, in their eagerness to propagate more heterogeneous churches, advocates of the multi-ethnic church either imply or state explicitly that the multi-ethnic church is God's ideal. In some cases, such passionate proponents declare that Scripture mandates multi-ethnic churches, and that anyone who disagrees with them is detracting from God's mission. For example, Bruce Fong in his book *Racial Equality in the Church* asserts that monocultural fellowships prioritize a particular culture over unity in Christ and therefore should be discouraged and multi-ethnic churches increased.[1] So too, Mark DeYmaz and Harry Li are quite explicit on this point:

> Some people will try to convince you that the multi-ethnic vision is not God's only plan for the church but simply one option. Still others will seek to discourage your efforts by wrongly interpreting your passion for the multi-ethnic church as a critique of their own segregated congregation. Such people will challenge your enthusiasm and your calling, much as Sanballat, Tobiah, and Geshem did in approaching Nehemiah. "They are trying to frighten us," Nehemiah recounts, "thinking, 'Their hands will get too weak for the work, and it will not be completed.' But I prayed, 'Now strengthen my hands'" (Neh. 6:9 [NIV 2011]). When you encounter such people, you too should pray, "Lord, strengthen my hands" and press on in pursuit of the vision God has given you.[2]

Such a view positions anyone who does not believe that the multi-ethnic church is God's *only* endorsed model for the local church as an enemy of the kingdom. We think that is a pretty harsh position to take when research finds only 4 percent of the churches in America are multi-ethnic.[3] Are

96 percent of churches in the United States really out of God's will? For that matter, were most of the churches over the past two thousand years of church history unbiblical simply because they were primarily mono-ethnic? We think not! From our perspective, mono-ethnic and multi-ethnic churches are both biblical models. Let us look at a short history of culture and ethnicity in the Old and New Testaments. What models emerge from these pages that would bring light to this controversial topic?

A SHORT HISTORY OF ETHNICITY

When did ethnicity and culture begin according to the biblical record? Author Miriam Adeney suggests they are rooted in God's nature. She writes, "God created us in his image, endowed us with creativity, and set us in a world of possibilities and challenges. Applying our God-given creativity, we have developed the cultures of the world."[4] But how did the cultures develop? What process did God use to bring ethnicity and culture about? While no one is completely sure, some clues emerge from the book of Genesis.

Following the initial story of Adam and Eve, we know that their children occupied various regions throughout the area and developed into large families. For instance, Genesis 4:17 indicates that Cain "built a city" for his family and descendants. We know that other of Adam's children married, had children, and established extended families as well. Genesis 5:1 begins, "This is the book of the generations of Adam," and then proceeds to name some of them: Seth, Enosh, Kenan, Mahalalel, Jared, Enoch, Methuselah, Lamech, and Noah.

Regrettably, significant numbers of Adam's descendants turned away from God, and humanity was reduced to Noah and his family through the flood. After that catastrophic event, we read, "From these the whole earth was populated" (Gen. 9:19). Genesis 10 is a celebration of the descendants of Noah who grew abundant and populated the entire known world.

Sometimes called the "Table of the Nations" by scholars, Genesis 10 bears witness to the fact that God was interested enough in each of these diverse peoples to record their names and groupings in the sacred text. The details of their existence were not lost on God. He knew them by name. He cared enough for them to preserve their memory. Most scholars also agree that elements of human culture—economic, social, and artistic— were developing. But then we encounter the sad story of the Tower of Babel in Genesis 11.

To some, the lesson extracted from this story is that the beginning of multiple cultures or ethnicities was a result of God's judgment. The scattering of the disobedient peoples into different languages is understood to be a curse that fragmented humanity and gave rise to the great diversity among peoples we see today. As some understand it, if diversity is a by-product of sin, then the intent of God's redemptive mission is to reverse the effects of the fall (Gen. 3) as seen in the judgment following the Tower of Babel, and restore unity and wholeness in Christ by bringing peoples back together in one multi-ethnic church.

Certainly the reversal of the fall is one of the great threads of the salvation story that plays itself out over the pages of the sacred text. In Christ, division is addressed and oneness becomes a hallmark of God's people. These are themes that are rightfully addressed by the multi-ethnic church. They become symbols of the restoration that is made possible by Jesus' work of redemption.

However, there is ample evidence that diversity is part of the created order and flows out of God's personal nature. The wide variety of birds, flowers, plants, and animal species are all uniquely crafted to bring glory to the designer who, out of his creativity and power, brought it all into existence. In the same way, each ethnicity, language, and culture is a unique expression of humanity made in the image of God. Each people group exhibits another way to bring glory to the Father. Thus, diversity is not a result of the judgment of God. Rather it is an outgrowth of his creative nature and therefore needs to be celebrated rather than eliminated through the uniformity created in some multi-ethnic churches.

Consider the diversity of language as an example of God's creativity. Linguistic anthropologists tell us that each language is not just a different way of saying the same thing. Often laypeople make the mistake of thinking that if we simply translate what we want to say into a different language we will communicate what we are thinking. The reality is that each language is a window into the worldview of a different people. Each language is a symbol set for a different way of thinking. Indonesians do not think like Americans but just happen to use different words. Indonesians actually think differently. They organize their world differently. They have a slightly different theology than North American believers—a unique understanding of God—because they come out of a different context, seeking to solve a slightly different set of questions. So, an Indonesian theology will likely be different than an American theology, and both can be theologically sound and biblically true.

Thus, there is another way to look at Genesis 10. One must take careful note that the Table of the Nations precedes the story of the Tower of Babel. Diversity was already present prior to the judgment at Babel. The scattering across the earth and the confusion of the languages was God's plan from the beginning. It was the human attempt at establishing a man-made unity that ran contrary to the purposes of God. So the judgment was a blessing in disguise, an affirmation that diversity is good and part of God's intention. Yet, the greater diversity is made up of smaller units and subunits that are all mono-ethnic! Multi-ethnic diversity literally cannot exist unless there are mono-ethnic subsets of peoples.

IN DEFENSE OF MONO-ETHNICITY

Several months ago on a trip to Costco, Alan watched a vendor demonstrating the superior qualities of a VitaMix machine. This is no ordinary blender! With its high-speed motor, it makes quick work of virtually anything that is thrown into it. No need to slice the carrots. Cut them in half (or not) and throw them in. Have a tomato? Take out the stem and throw it in. Do you have half an onion, a handful of spinach, any leftover vegetables? Throw in a random assortment of anything you can imagine. The machine mixes them all.

The man behind the counter said the VitaMix is even a good way to get children to eat their vegetables. Making your kids a strawberry smoothie? Add some spinach. They will never know the difference. The bottom line: if you can eat it, you can drink it! Just mix it up with your VitaMix machine, add enough liquid, and anything will go down.

Inspired, Alan went home with a new machine and huge aspirations. Over time, however, he noticed that when so many options are mixed up, no one taste stands out and the usual color is brown! When drinking the concoction, there is a sense that what one is drinking is healthy, but indistinct and not nearly as pleasing as experiencing each fruit or vegetable as God intended it.

We don't know about you, but we enjoy the unique qualities of fruits and vegetables when they are in season and at their best state of freshness. There is nothing like a good, ripe strawberry, and we marvel at the Creator's genius in making it. The fact of the matter is that diversity is good, and it brings out the richness of life. Fruit salad tastes better when the apples, oranges, and strawberries are distinct, while yet flavoring each other.

But a review of Scripture seems to suggest permission and in some cases even a preference for a monocultural gathering of believers! Certainly a repeated injunction given to Israel in the Old Testament is to come out from among the nations and be holy (Lev. 20:26; Ezra 10:11). When they inter-mingled with the nations, they were judged for unfaithfulness. If anything, in the Old Testament, it seems that mono-culturalism[5] was commanded and enforced.

In the New Testament church, the emphasis seems to move from erecting barriers keeping out cultural intrusions to removing the cultural barriers to faith that impede the growth of the church. Dirke Johnson notes that the New Testament seems to shift the focus at the Council of Jerusalem (Acts 15).

The underlying principle expressed at the Council was, "We should not make it difficult for the Gentiles who are turning to God" (Acts 15:19 [NIV]). The Council of Jerusalem's decision may speak louder by what they did not say than by what they did say. The Gentiles were given permission to not adopt a Jewish cultural expression of faith and the Jewish believers are not asked to change their cultural expression of faith either. This would seem to have been the opportune time to identify exactly how Jews and Gentiles would exhibit their oneness by a particular way of doing things or insisting that they do them together, there is a freedom of ecclesiology that allows distinct cultural practices of Christianity.[6]

As one looks toward the future, the church in Revelation 7:9–10 stands as a picture of where history is headed: "After these things I looked, and behold, a great multitude which no one could count, from every nation and *all* tribes and peoples and tongues, standing before the throne and before the Lamb, clothed in white robes, and palm branches *were* in their hands; and they cry out with a loud voice, saying, 'Salvation to our God who sits on the throne, and to the Lamb.'"

Clearly, in the future kingdom, the distinctiveness of each ethnic culture and language is not lost. Each mono-ethnic group is a window into the greatness of God, declaring his glory in its own way.

For most of us, it is counterintuitive to go against the way we were raised. The cultural values that were embedded into our consciousness from an early age are held unconsciously, intuitively. We naturally think that our way of seeing the world is the best way of seeing it, the only right way of seeing it. This preference for one's own culture functions in healthy ways to give us a mental map for navigating our world.

This level of our culture is deeply embedded and slow to change. Unless our mental map is challenged through cross-cultural exposure or alternative worldviews, like one would likely encounter in urban contexts, it remains intact. To act contrary to our culture requires relearning and often deliberate effort. Even then, we tend to revert back to previously held models unless we are exposed to new ways of thinking long enough. This process of changing our worldview assumptions is not instinctive and is difficult.

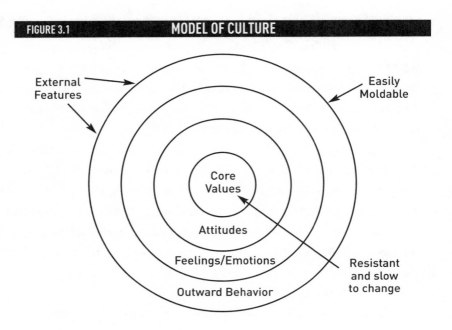

FIGURE 3.1   **MODEL OF CULTURE**

External Features

Easily Moldable

Core Values

Attitudes

Feelings/Emotions

Outward Behavior

Resistant and slow to change

The trajectory of Old Testament history changes in Genesis 12. Rather than treating humanity as a whole, beginning with Abraham the message of salvation is mediated through the few—Abraham and his descendants. The blessing promised to Abraham in Genesis 12:1–3 is given with a wider expressed purpose, "And I will make you a great nation, And I will bless you, And make your name great; And *so you shall be a blessing*; And I will bless those who bless you, And the one who curses you I will curse. And *in you all the families of the earth will be blessed*" (Gen. 12:2–3, emphasis added). Note the intention of the blessing in the words italicized above. It is clearly given for the purpose of blessing the nations, or in other words, the other cultures and ethnicities in the world.

There are, of course, negative aspects of being embedded in one's culture. For instance, most people view their culture as the best one. This preference for one's own culture is called ethnocentrism, and it has both good and bad aspects. From the positive side, it provides a way to navigate through one's culture and world, but from a negative perspective, it results in exclusivist attitudes that end up in rejection of other peoples. The exclusivism that naturally follows ethnocentrism is rejected in Abraham's promise:

> The salvation of the nations was God's ultimate motivation in making Abraham's name great and in being the God of Abraham's innumerable progeny. This universal purpose totally dominates the covenant. . . . God stresses in various ways his promise of hope to the nations of the world (Gen. 18:17, 18; 22:18; 26:4; 28:14). Centuries later the apostle Paul calls this promise nothing less than the gospel: "The Scripture foresaw that God would justify the Gentiles by faith, and announced the gospel in advance to Abraham: 'All nations will be blessed through you'" (Gal. 3:8).[7]

Years later, Israel's deliverance from Egypt was to indelibly impress upon them a special sensitivity and compassion for the sojourner, the alien, and the dispossessed. In addition to showing justice to slaves (Gen. 17:12; 37:28), caring for widows (Ex. 22:22–24; Deut. 10:18; 24:17–21; Mal. 3:5), and redistributing land instead of accumulating wealth (Lev. 25:8–17), Israel was to protect the minority peoples in its midst. Non-Israelites who came to dwell among the people of Israel were to have rights and privileges. Mission theologian Arthur Glasser points out that these minority peoples were to enjoy the rest of the Sabbath (Ex. 23:12), be given opportunity to glean from the fields (Lev. 19:9–10; 23:22), and be included in the provisions for the cities of refuge (Num. 35:15).[8]

> Because they were defenseless, God promised to be their defense and the judge of those who oppressed them (Jer. 7:6; 22:3). The sojourner, or resident alien, was virtually on the level with the Israelite (Lev. 24:22), and in Ezekiel's vision of the messianic age they are to share the inheritance of Israel (Ezek. 47:22–23 . . .). The extended emphasis in the Old Testament on the "stranger within the gates" means that the church-in-mission today must give priority to the needs of all minority and immigrant peoples, an issue particularly important today

with regard to the millions of displaced and refugee people we find all over the globe.[9]

The people of Israel were commanded to include other mono-ethnic peoples, even while they were to pursue the maintenance of their own culture and ethnic identity. An exploration of the Wisdom Literature (see Pss. 2, 33, 66, 67, 72, 89, 98, 117, 145) and the Prophets (Isa. 42:6, 49:6; and the book of Jonah) reveals God's heart for the nations both inside and outside Israel's borders. While the Israelites were to cultivate an allegiance to Yahweh and regularly celebrate how he had intervened in their history, they nevertheless had a stewardship responsibility to invite the nations to join them in worship and enact justice and respect for those of other cultures. This truth is unmistakable in the pages of the Old Testament.

We discover in the New Testament that Jesus started out decidedly focused on mono-ethnic ministry to Israel. In Mark 7:24–30 and Matthew 15:22–28, he encountered the Syro-Phoenecian woman whose daughter had an unclean spirit. When she asked him to heal her daughter, his initial response was one of reluctance saying to her, "'Let the children be satisfied first, for it is not good to take the children's bread and throw it to the dogs.' But she answered and said to Him, 'Yes, Lord, *but* even the dogs under the table feed on the children's crumbs'" (Mark 7:27–28). This striking passage has led some scholars to conclude that Jesus never intended a ministry beyond Israel or only later added this objective to his ministry goals.

Such a theory seems made more plausible by the command Jesus gave his disciples in Matthew 10:5–10. Sometimes called the "limited commission," Jesus instructed them, "Do not go in *the* way of *the* Gentiles, and do not enter *any* city of the Samaritans; but rather go to the lost sheep of the house of Israel" (Matt. 10:5–6). To solve the problems presented by these passages, most evangelical scholars explain that Jesus, as the promised Messiah, first had the responsibility to call Israel back to repentance and right standing before God before he could urge the people to carry the gospel to the nations. Then too, while these passages would seem to suggest that Jesus endorsed an exclusive, mono-ethnic orientation, his own life and ministry demonstrated this was not the case. Even in his early ministry Jesus demonstrated his love, and thus Israel's responsibility, for the foreigner. He healed the Syro-Phoenician woman's daughter (Mark 7:24–30) and the Roman centurion's son (John 4:46–53). He ministered to the deep needs of the woman at the well (John 4), a member of the despised, half-breed Samaritans. He cast the demons out of the Gadarene demoniacs in Matthew 8. And beginning in Matthew 24 and Mark 13 he spoke of the task his disciples would be given to take the gospel to the nations. What is clear from these and other passages is that, while Jesus did not advocate that one must give up his or her heritage and culture in order to follow him, there nevertheless must be an inclusiveness that embraces those of other cultures as inheritors of the blessings of Abraham.

This truth is further borne out in the book of Acts. Though there were people from every nation who witnessed the miracle of Pentecost in Acts 2, the earliest church was largely captive to Jerusalem (Acts 2:41; 8:1). To free the gospel from this cultural captivity, it took repeated and deliberate interventions of the Holy Spirit to spread it beyond the borders of Jerusalem. In Acts 6:1–7, it spread to the Jews with Greek culture (Hellenists); in 8:4–24 to the Samaritans; in 8:26–40 to the Gentiles with Jewish beliefs (as with the Ethiopian eunuch); in Acts 10–11 to the god-fearers; in chapters 13–14 to the Gentiles with Greco-Roman culture; and again in chapter 15 to both Jews and Gentiles with Greek and Hebrew cultural backgrounds. As Dirke Johnson noted earlier, these cultures were not simply fused together with their uniqueness eliminated. Rather, each was valued independently and by the gifts they could contribute to enlarge the understanding of God.

At the Council of Jerusalem in Acts 15, neither the Jewish nor the Gentile believers were asked to forsake their cultural uniqueness but were allowed to worship God in their own way, recognizing that God had revealed himself differently to these diverse peoples.

Both Scripture (especially the book of Acts) and history show us that the gospel spreads most easily once the message is incarnated into a worldview and culture. Once a viable nucleus of believers is strong and well organized enough to begin an independent evangelism effort, the gospel spreads more easily. However, the gospel naturally stops spreading when it encounters cultural, linguistic, geographical, and economic barriers. To get over these barriers usually requires deliberate effort or an act of the Spirit.[10] The historical sketch of the growth of the church found in Acts demonstrates that God did not eliminate mono-ethnic groups, but actually worked through each group to reach the world. The gospel spread as it became fixed in each separate monocultural unit and subunit of society.

IN PURSUIT OF MULTI-ETHNICITY

Exclusive monoculturalism (or exclusive mono-ethnicity) is not a viable option for God's people. We can, though, affirm the value and uniqueness of each culture and at the same time reject a retreat into exclusive monoculturalism that neglects the responsibilities we have as stewards of the gospel of the kingdom. As we were once strangers and aliens to God, we must now welcome those from other cultures into our fellowships locally, just as we also must cross boundaries to take the gospel to those outside our cultural and geographical contexts.

We have an even greater responsibility than to simply welcome diverse peoples into our mono-ethnic fellowships. Advocates of the multi-ethnic church point to passages such as John 17, the book of Acts, and Ephesians 3 to make a case for why the church must be multi-ethnic in order to be biblically faithful. In John 17:20–23 we read:

> I do not ask on behalf of these alone, but for those also who believe in Me through their word; that they may all be one; even as You, Father, *are* in Me and I in You, that they also may be in Us, so that the world may believe that You sent Me. The glory which You have given Me I have given to them, that they may be one, just as We are one; I in them and You in Me, that they may be perfected in unity, so that the world may know that You sent Me, and loved them, even as You have loved Me.

What is clear from this passage is that unity among believers becomes a powerful witness to the world regarding the reconciling work of the gospel. The breaking of relationships (between man and God, man and man, man and creation, and even man within himself) is a result of the fall and is caused by the selfishness and sin that lurks inside all of us. That division between others and us is manifested in racism, divorce, exploitation of the weak, and abuse of the environment. So, as these relationships are restored by Christ's Spirit within us, the world knows that a miracle has occurred and that God lives. The healing of broken relationships is an essential message of the kingdom.

What is not clear from these verses is whether such healing and unity is necessarily expressed in the establishment of multi-ethnic churches, though the healing of animosity and division between ethnicities and cultures is certainly part of the reconciliation that must occur. Healing may occur in several different forms. The tearing down of the divisions among ethnicities is critical, but that does not have to happen in the form of a multi-ethnic church. Monocultural churches should not be thought of as automatically opposed to Scripture. Dirke Johnson points out that people may choose to participate in a monocultural gathering whether it be an independent church, a congregation, or a small group within a larger church for reasons other than those motivated by racism and sin: "Monocultural settings are not selected out of animosity toward other cultures but usually because one feels they best connect with God and that particular family of believers. A study done in 2000 by Emerson and Smith revealed that prejudice is not a motivator for Blacks to attend predominantly Black churches. They identify the culprits that encourage monocultural gatherings as social and religious pluralism. The American religious system is designed on choice and competition. The implication is that the majority of people choose monocultural gatherings for positive and not negative reasons."[11]

It is possible that the unity spoken of in John 17 could be expressed in the breaking down of ethnic division without necessarily forming a multi-ethnic church in which there is no racial majority. John 17 leaves no doubt that animosity, prejudice, or racism that divides people of different ethnic groups has no place in God's kingdom. However, it does not exclude the possibility that ethnic division can be addressed while attending a mono-ethnic church. John 17 simply is not that specific (more discussion on this is found in chapter 8).

Another passage that is often cited as giving support for the multi-ethnic church is Ephesians chapters 2 and 3. In these chapters, Paul talked about the reconciliation of mankind with the Father (chapter 2) and reconciliation between the Jew and Gentile (chapter 3). Again, the passage speaks author-itatively that the divisions that once divided people and that characterized our lives under sin must be eradicated as we pursue life in Christ. Whether the "mystery of Christ" spoken of in 3:3–4 is the gospel or the reconcilia-tion between ethnic groups is not totally clear from the passage, but that unity among believers will be a hallmark of the faith is not in question. Diversity, whether expressed in terms of ethnicity, gender, socioeconomic status, language, education, or something else must be celebrated and given voice, and not allowed to divide.

Believing that differences should not divide is good theology but con-siderably more difficult to practice. As the church developed in the book of Acts, we have already seen that the natural tendencies of the human heart displayed a certain ignorance, reluctance, or disinterest to take the gospel beyond one's ethnic group. Apart from deliberate acts of the Holy Spirit, the Jews might still have dominated the church. The gospel spread to Hellenized Jews, the Samaritans, the Gentile God-fearers, and eventually to the ends of the earth because the Holy Spirit, or Holy Spirit-empowered believers, delib-erately crossed ethnic boundaries to include those who would have other-wise been excluded. The model held up in the book of Acts is one of diversity brought together in unity because of the power of the gospel. That diversity goes beyond simply mixing ethnic diversity. It also extends to the types and range of churches that are biblically faithful. The diagram below seeks to capture this discussion in a graphic format.

BIBLICAL AND NONBIBLICAL RESPONSES TO MULTI-ETHNICITY

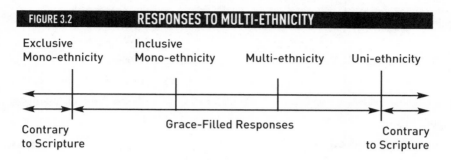

FIGURE 3.2   RESPONSES TO MULTI-ETHNICITY

At both ends of this continuum are models of church that are not biblically supported. A mono-ethnicity that excludes outsiders (by intention or neglect) or takes lightly its stewardship responsibility to share the gospel with the nations falls into the trap the people of Israel found themselves in when they did not realize they were blessed in order to be a blessing. At the opposite end, a uni-ethnicity that so blends everyone together so that God's unique cultural expression in them is lost (the VitaMix illustration) is unbiblical also. In Acts 15, neither the Jews nor the Gentiles were mandated to depart from their cultural moorings in order to be part of the family of faith.

However, the two church models in the middle of the diagram, the largely mono-ethnic church that consciously reaches out and includes the minority believer, as well as the more truly multi-ethnic church that seeks to become multi-ethnic (and multicultural) in every aspect of church life are true to the teachings of John 17 and Ephesians 2–3. Both of these models seek to disciple and educate new believers as to the implications of their new faith. Once a new believer begins to experience relational reconciliation and growth in sanctification, it becomes increasingly necessary for him or her to become proactive in bridging the ethnic divides that are common in society at large. We believe this can take place in both mono-ethnic and multi-ethnic churches. Neither has exclusive claim to be the only model God uses.

Having recognized that the crossing of boundaries is necessary as a steward of the gospel, the question becomes how and to what extent? As we have seen from chapter 2 of this book, multi-ethnicity generally means that multiple ethnicities attend the same church. Some churches consider John 17 and Ephesians 2–3 fulfilled only if they are locally multi-ethnic at any level or amount. For others this is inadequate, and they believe that a multi-ethnic worship service is required to be faithful to God's vision. Still others insist that the small group ministry, the church leadership, even leadership styles should be multi-ethnic. Others consider it sufficiently fulfilled if they are part of a denomination or fellowship of churches that are composed of multiple ethnicities.

We believe that the biblical response is to embrace differences while respecting the uniqueness of each culture as an expression of God's creative purposes. The primary goal is to work toward greater unity and oneness between ethnicities (as well as with other types of diversity such as economic, gender, and generational diversity) in whatever model of church with which we are working.

There is more than one way to do this. Thus, all of the models are right in one sense.

PUTTING INSIGHTS TO WORK

1. Do you think a local church must be multi-ethnic to be considered biblical? Why or why not?

2. What makes a church multi-ethnic? How much blending or mixing of ethnicities must be in place for a church to be genuinely multi-ethnic?

3. May a local church be mono-ethnic and still fulfill God's desire for unity among believers? Why or why not? How might be happen?

4
OUR MOBILE WORLD

In this new century and new millennium we are seeing the greatest movement of humanity around the globe ever seen in human history.
—Charles Van Engen

The history of the world is the history of people on the move. It is an old story told in many different ways. One familiar story recounts how one member of a family, usually a man, migrates to a different part of the world in search of a better future. After years of hard work, eventually the entire family follows, establishing the family or entire clan in a new country. The story of Joseph is one such story. After Joseph's brothers sold him into slavery in Egypt, God providentially promoted Joseph to a place of authority where he could save his entire family from starvation. Years after the family moved to Egypt and increased greatly, they migrated back to the Promised Land. Joseph's story is one of forced migration, but millions of people have also relocated voluntarily throughout history.

Migration takes place for a number of reasons. The United Nations estimated that in 2009 43.3 million people were forcibly displaced.[1] Of these, 27.1 million migrated within their country of origin, while 16.2 million moved beyond their original place of residence. Other millions migrate of their own free choice from rural to urban environments in search of a better life. In 1800 only 3 percent of the world's population lived in cities. By

1900 the total was 14 percent, and that increased to 30 percent by 1950. Over the last half century, migration to urban centers has been unprecedented, with 50 percent of world population living in cities in 2008. Rural to urban migration is not slowing down, and it is estimated that by 2050, 70 percent of the world's population will be living in cities. As missiologist Ray Bakke noted a quarter century ago, "The Lord is urbanizing his world."[2] Add together the voluntary and involuntary migration of people, and at least fifty million people, likely many more, are in movement somewhere in the world at any given time.[3]

The American hemisphere—North, Central, and South—is characterized by migration. Since the fifteenth century, when early explorers ventured into this part of the world from Europe, migration has gradually increased. Today's movement of people goes far beyond the relocation of people to the United States. The main destination of people from Mexico, Canada, and Venezuela is the United States. However, the primary destination of Columbians is Venezuela. People moving out of Bolivia prefer to go to Argentina. People are even migrating out of the United States, with the top five destinations being Mexico, Canada, Puerto Rico, the United Kingdom, and the Philippines.[4]

EVANGELISM AND CHURCH GROWTH

The Christian church is directly linked to the natural movement of human populations to and from the urban centers of the ancient world. Jerusalem, Antioch, Corinth, Athens, and Rome are just a few of the urban cities where the gospel took root. At the beginning of the church in Acts 2, people were gathered in Jerusalem from every corner of the known world (Acts 2:8–11). After the Holy Spirit empowered the church for witness, these people returned to their homes preaching the good news of Jesus Christ. The disciples and particularly the apostle Paul, moved from urban center to urban center evangelizing receptive peoples. Urban mobility had great impact on the growth of the early church. In the coming half-century, an even larger movement of people into the cities of the world will have increasing significance for the growth of the church in the future. Why is this so?

Cities Are Where People Live

Closely related to the migration of peoples around the world is the growth of urban centers—cities and megacities. While there is no commonly accepted definition of an urban city, it is generally assumed that cities of twenty-five hundred or more residents, which are not dependent on an agricultural economy, are urban. As urban cities grow into contact with each other, they form agglomerations, or urban centers of one million or more residents. In 1900 only twelve cities in the world had populations of over one million, but just fifty years later there were eighty-three such cities. Today, there are over four hundred cities with a population of a million or more and nineteen megacities with over ten million. By 2025 it is expected that twenty-one cities will be megacities. There is no better place to reach people than the urban centers of our world.

The gospel is about people. As God's church, we are on a mission to preach the gospel of salvation to all nations. There is no better place to do so than in the urban centers of the world. As missiologist Donald McGavran commented, "The assignment is not 'to reach the cities.' The Church has already done that. Her task is to bring urban multitudes to faith and obedience."[5]

Change Causes People to Be Open to the Gospel

It is a fact of life that "the receptivity or responsiveness of individuals waxes and wanes."[6] People vary in their openness to Christ. A few years ago, a church in southern California divided its city into three sections and then proceeded to target each section with its outreach efforts. Over a year's time, the leaders kept careful account of the responses to the gospel from each section. At the end of one year, church leaders took note that one section of the city showed a higher response than the other two. After further analysis, it was discovered that the unresponsive areas of the city were comprised of people who had lived in their homes for ten or more years, while the responsive area was comprised of young families and singles that had recently moved into the city. Correctly, the church concluded that new move-ins were more responsive than those who had lived in the area for many years.

Research has determined that the most common indicator of receptivity is when people experience change in their lives. Change happens when people migrate to a new place. Church planters have known for years that the best place to start a new church is in a new community. Why is this so? The recent arrivals have experienced a great deal of change and are open to new relationships. New move-ins must search for fresh places to shop, new doctors, hairdressers, friends, and in many instances, a new faith.

Conflict also makes some people receptive to the gospel. Following World War II (1939–1945) and the Korean Conflict (1950–1953), the Korean people became highly receptive to the gospel. As a result, the church in Korea grew mightily for fifty years, and in the process, saw the establishment of some of the world's largest churches.

Newfound freedom also leads some people to a fresh encounter with Christ. Church ministries that minister on college and university campuses build on the receptivity of new students. Young students who are away from home for the first time and thrust into an environment where they question everything are often highly receptive to the gospel. The freedom of being able to question old assumptions, inquire into fresh ideas, and explore new roads of life creates openness to the gospel.

As newcomers face acculturation into a new culture, they encounter changes that open them up to new ways of thinking. Nothing challenges a person's thinking like that of wrestling with a new culture. Recent immigrants to a country are some of the most receptive people in the world, and they often live in urban centers.

Urban Centers Break Down Barriers

If a multi-ethnic church is going to grow and thrive, it will do so most readily in urban centers of the world. Even there, however, it is true that "birds of a feather flock together." That is, peoples of common language, ancestry, origin, and history find it beneficial to band together for support, encouragement, and protection. Since it is common for people to band together, mono-ethnic churches are necessary if we hope to reach them for Christ. Congregations must fit the ethnic, cultural, economic, physical, and social characteristics of the people (the *ethne*) being reached. In fact mono-ethnic churches are the most common type of church and will continue to be so, even in the face of growing interest in multi-ethnic churches.

However, as people are thrown tightly together, mixed as it were in the hotbed of urban centers, the natural aspects of life that separate various people are worn away, allowing for gathering of different peoples into multi-ethnic churches. This becomes particularly true of second- and third-generation immigrants.

ETHNIC IDENTIFICATION

Ethnic bonds have always existed among communities of people maintaining their identity through national origin, religion, and ethnic consciousness. Such bonds take on a complex mixture related to cultural connection and desire for assimilation into the host culture. An individual's cultural connectedness can be broken into three categories.

C-1 = People with a particularly strong cultural identity. They speak their heart language fluently (perhaps only) and greatly enjoy engaging in all the cultural aspects of their heritage (music, food, stories, history, etc.).

C-2 = People who have an appreciation for their ethnic culture and the dominant culture. They often speak two languages and feel comfortable moving back and forth from one cultural context to another.

C-3 = People with a low intensity of ethnic consciousness. They strongly identify with the dominant culture and are happy participating in organizations made up of people from outside their historical ethnic identity.

Another aspect of ethnic consciousness relates to the way the desire of persons from one culture to assimilate into a new dominant culture varies along three distinct categories.

A-1 = People who have no desire to assimilate into the dominant culture. They view assimilation as unnecessary or simply do not want to put out the effort it takes to learn a new language and cultural forms.

A-2 = People who feel comfortable in two different cultural contexts. They often engage one cultural context in work, school, or other outside experiences, while engaging their primary cultural experience through extended family relationships.

A-3 = People who evidence a strong desire to fully assimilate into the dominant culture. Involvement with their ethnic culture takes place occasionally through family gatherings, historical investigation, and memories of grandparents.

By combining an individual's intensity for cultural identification with his or her desire for assimilation, we are able to define three major possibilities for social involvement.

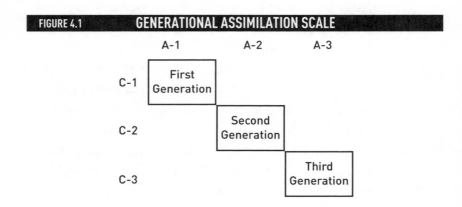

FIGURE 4.1   **GENERATIONAL ASSIMILATION SCALE**

Understanding this graphic brings out several important insights. Mono-ethnic churches begin with a population in the C-1 and A-1 category. These churches flourish for thirty to forty years if the immigration of first generation people stops, but longer if immigration continues and/or cultural identity remains intense. First generation peoples who are immersed in the country and culture of their origin find it comforting to band together in mono-ethnic churches for support, assistance, and protection as they engage the dominant cultural environment of the new nation to which they have migrated. Evangelizing these new people requires either the planting of mono-ethnic churches or the establishment of a mono-ethnic congregation within another church.

As a second generation begins to emerge (C-2 and A-2), mono-ethnic churches start to function as two-in-one churches. This is most visible in the use of two languages in one worship service, with translation of the native language being given in the host language. As leadership is passed to the second generation, the church usually begins offering two different worship services with one in the mother language and cultural forms, and one in the dominant culture's language and cultural forms. Typically, the generation most interested in being part of a multi-ethnic church is the second generation of C-2s and A-2s. They feel comfortable being in two different worlds, sort of like having one foot each in two different cultures. They know how to get along in each culture, find the tension invigorating, and enjoy navigating the complexity of different cultures.

Members of the third generation (C-3 and A-3) quite often prefer to assimilate in host culture churches. However, if they have experienced racism or find it difficult to assimilate into the dominant culture, they may desire participation in a multi-ethnic church that focuses on reconciliation. With the emergence of a third generation, some young leaders break away to start ethnic-American churches totally in the form of the dominant culture. Other people of the third generation break away and assimilate with churches in the dominant culture.

The fourth generation and beyond usually assimilates into the host culture of a country to the point of not being much aware of its heritage. This has been the case of countless people who trace their ancestry to Poland,

France, Ireland, Russia, Germany, and a host of other countries. This is especially true of people who cannot easily return to their country of origin. Other peoples, however, due to economic depression, connection to their original country, racial discrimination, or high ethnic consciousness resist assimilation into the host culture and remain in a sort of continuous C-2 and A-2 limbo. These members of the fourth generation occasionally spur a movement to restore their language and culture. Such was the "black is beautiful" movement of a number of years ago or the current popularity of Native Americans relearning ancient languages, crafts, and religious practices. Forth generation people may also be prime candidates for involvement in a multi-ethnic church that respects and includes elements of their primal culture. But in cases where the desire to return to one's original culture is strongly emphasized, as in some Native American tribes, there may be an increased resistance to multi-ethnic churches.

WHAT DO WE NEED TO DO?

With this basic understanding of ethnic consciousness, it should be apparent that building multi-ethnic churches is a complex undertaking. So what do we need to do?

Do the Research

Urban evangelism and church planting will not happen without solid research. Years ago, Roger Greenway wrote, "The highest and best mission leaders often spend more time devising strategies to reach [one hundred] tribal cavemen in some remote corner of earth than to reach the urban millions—apartment house dwellers, slum residents, and new rural-urban migrants—and multiply churches among them."[7] The best multi-ethnic churches arise from a wise and practical understanding of a city, community, or neighborhood. Some areas may be ripe for a multi-ethnic church, but in other areas the most fruitful evangelism may be accomplished by planting mono-ethnic churches. Solid research on the context and peoples in a target area will produce the best results.

Focus on Receptive Peoples

The goal is not to plant one type of church over a different type of church, but to plant a church that will make disciples. An urban center is comprised of different groups of people—a mosaic of hundreds of segments of society. Those seeking to start a church, after research, should focus on the segment felt to be the most responsive. After a year, however, if five new converted families have not been reached and formed into a church, it may be wise to seek a more receptive area or mosaic of the population.

Welcome the Stranger

One of the primary concepts of an immigrant in the Bible is that of a stranger. God instructed the people of Israel to treat strangers well. For example, God said, "When a stranger resides with you in your land, you shall not do him wrong. The stranger who resides with you shall be to you as the native among you, and you shall love him as yourself, for you were aliens in the land of Egypt; I am the LORD your God" (Lev. 19:33–34).

A stranger, alien, or immigrant is generally thought of as "the marginalized, the needy, the minority groups, and those who are under-represented in social, political, and economic arenas."[8] It is clear that part of God's mission in the world is for churches to be welcoming communities of faith that do not mistreat outsiders. Churches must care for strangers just as they would for one of their own. Why should this be? We, as Christians, are strangers and pilgrims on this earth, just like Israel was a stranger in Egypt. Again, it does not matter if the church is mono-ethnic or multi-ethnic; strangers are to be welcome.

Plant Churches—Mono-Ethnic and Multi-Ethnic

Nonbelievers are not going around seeking a mono-ethnic or a multi-ethnic church. The reality is that most secular people are not searching for any kind of church. Churches that intentionally reach out to the non-churched in their communities with love, grace, and understanding, will be fruitful. In some cases churches demonstrating an uncommon blending of ethnic groups will be the most fruitful, while in other neighborhoods, churches that worship with one cultural style will no doubt be most effective. It will take all kinds of churches to reach all kinds of people. To assume that one approach will reach every person ignores the reality of people's differences. We are for mono-ethnic and multi-ethnic churches, as well as traditional and nontraditional, contemporary and ancient. Reaching the millions of urban dwellers will take many kinds of churches.

Champion House Churches

House churches typically arise during times of persecution and revival. Since the North American culture is not experiencing either of these two aspects of life, it is doubtful that house churches will gain a major foothold in the culture in the near future. Yet the economic stresses being experienced by many may indeed lead to house churches forming so that people may walk to church rather than drive. This may be seen particularly in urban centers where land values prohibit a small cell of Christians from purchasing land and building a traditional place of worship. Instead of placing a heavy burden on a small congregation, it will be best for a church to meet in the most natural surroundings to which non-Christians may come with the greatest of ease, and in many situations this will be a home in the neighborhood. However, it is likely that most house churches will tend toward being mono-ethnic rather than multi-ethnic. Research by professor Scott Thumma of Hartford Seminary in Connecticut demonstrated that larger congregations as a whole are better at reaching multi-ethnic peoples.[9] It is almost a truism that the smaller the church the more mono-ethnic its makeup, and the larger the church the more multi-ethnic its makeup. Thus, if we desire to see more multi-ethnic congregations, we need to see larger churches too.

The mobility of millions of people around the world is creating great challenges and opportunities. As millions of people migrate around the world in the coming decades and become compressed into the urban centers, multi-ethnic churches are likely to become more prevalent. Yet mono-ethnic churches will continue to be needed, particularly for recent immigrants and those with a high people-consciousness (a concept that is discussed at length in the next chapter).

PUTTING INSIGHTS TO WORK

1. Have you observed any people movements in your community? Describe what you have seen.

2. In what way have you seen the movement of people along the Generational Assimilation Scale? If your family has a history of migration, how does it fit on this scale?

3. Which of the five ideas noted under "What Do We Need to Do?" can you put into practice in your own church?

IMMIGRANTS AND CHURCHES IN THE USA

*These States are the amplest poem, Here is not merely
a nation but a teeming Nation of nations.*
—Walt Whitman

The signs are unmistakable. The United States is becoming . . . no . . . Is multi-ethnic! Headlines announce the reality of our national diversity almost daily in newspapers, magazines, on television, and the Internet. For example, a front page article in *USA Today* declared, "Diversity Grows as Majority Dwindles: Minorities Make up Almost Half of Births."[1] While this headline did not catch too many North Americans by surprise, perhaps the headline of *The Californian* a year earlier did when it announced its New Year baby: "It's a Boy: Son of Pakistani immigrants is Southwest County's first baby."

The baby boy was born in Murrieta, California, a second-ring suburb of Los Angeles. This baby is too young to know it now, but one of these days he will learn his family's story sounds like millions of immigrant stories. His grandfather, a jeweler, left Pakistan twenty years ago to forge a better life in the United States. In the first few years, the family remained behind in Pakistan while his grandfather established a career in a new land. Without his family, and with little income, he was only able to call his wife for ten minutes each week. Slowly over several years, one by one, he brought his family to the United States. He worked at a gas station to make ends meet, and became a citizen in 1991. In his spare time he studied to become a certified diamond expert. In an interview, he expressed his reasons for moving to the United States, "I want to do the best for my children, give them the best opportunity for an education in the United States, the best country in the world."[2]

This family's story could be repeated by numerous people—Irish, Chinese, Polish, Costa Rican, Iranian, etc. One of the unique aspects of North American culture is that, except for Native Americans and many African-Americans, almost everyone came here because they wanted to come.

A SHORT HISTORY OF IMMIGRATION IN THE UNITED STATES

US historian Oscar Handlin once observed that writing the history of the United States meant writing the history of immigration. Archaeological research suggests that even the Native American peoples of the American continent came from elsewhere. Some researchers suggest that the ancient wave of immigrants came some ten thousand to twenty thousand years ago when hunters and nomads crossed the Bering Strait from Asia and began making their way south. Others claim peoples crossing the Pacific Ocean and then making their way north first settled Latin America.

Early Arrivals

We now know for a fact that Vikings arrived about A.D. 1000, nearly five hundred years before European exploration started. From 1500 on, conquistadors, voyageurs, merchants, priests, and slave traders brought people to the new world voluntarily and involuntarily, forever changing the face of North America.

European migration started about 1607, and the Pilgrims (102 English colonists) arrived in 1620 on the *Mayflower*. These colonists were motivated, in part, by the desire for religious freedom. This is generally considered to be the start of planned European migration. The establishment of the first Dutch colony on Manhattan Island took place in 1624. However, the Dutch did not come to the new world for reasons of religious liberty, but rather for the pursuit of commerce. The Swedes came in 1638. They were not religious dissenters, but were an organized group of colonizers sent by the Swedish government to establish a colony in Delaware.

The population of the early colonies that later became the United States grew from zero Europeans in the mid-1550s, to 3.2 million Europeans and seven hundred thousand African slaves by 1790. It is estimated that about three-fourths of the population at that time were of British descent, with Germans forming 7 percent. The remainder was a mosaic of Dutch, Swedish, Scotch-Irish, and others.

Official United States Immigration

After the founding of the United States, the country gradually developed its immigration policy. The Naturalization Act of 1790 stipulated, "Any alien, being a free white person, may be admitted to become a citizen of the United States." Thomas Jefferson supervised the first census in the US and three categories were available for people to indicate their origins: free white males, free white females, and other (free blacks, Indians, and slaves). This first census institutionalized the practice of labeling people by race. Around three hundred thousand African slaves arrived in North America before United States independence, with an additional one hundred thousand coming between 1776 and 1860.

Most of the early immigrants came from countries in Europe. About 1.8 million Irish immigrants came during the famous Great Potato Famine in the mid-1800s, with five hundred thousand Germans arriving between 1800 and 1850. Some twenty thousand Germans came between 1816 and 1817, fleeing a famine, while another sixty thousand fled to North America after the failed revolutions of 1848. Germans continued to come and, between 1850 and 1930, five million entered the US, reaching a peak between 1881 and 1885. Not everyone came from Europe, with nine hundred thousand French Canadians leaving Canada to emigrate to the United States over nearly a century (1840–1930), settling mostly in New England.

On January 2, 1892, a new federal immigration station opened on Ellis Island in New York Harbor. Italian immigration reached a high point between 1910 and 1920, when over two million came to the United States. The 1900s saw immigration driven by violent forces exploding in Europe and the collapse of colonial empires. The 1917 Russian Revolution, World War I, the upheavals in Nazi Germany during the late 1930s till the end of World War II, the Spanish Civil War (1936–1939), and the Cuban revolution all had a profound impact on immigration to the United States. The immigration of tens of thousands of Cubans to the United States following Fidel Castro's 1959 revolution changed the face of Miami, Florida, and Newark, New Jersey.

Changing Patterns of Immigration

A period of free immigration took place between the 1800 and 1870. The Chinese were the first Asians to arrive in the United States in large numbers. By 1830 Chinese people were selling goods in New York City and working in sugarcane fields in Hawaii.

Discovery of gold in California in 1848 attracted thousands of Chinese miners and laborers, and by 1860 nearly thirty-seven thousand Chinese had immigrated to California. The Central Pacific Railroad recruited Chinese in 1865, and in 1868 the United States opened its doors to even greater Chinese immigration through the Burlingame Treaty.

For half a century, from 1880 to 1940, a period of anti-Asian immigration, particularly against Chinese, existed in the United States. Immigration patterns prior to 1880 swelled the Chinese population to sixty-five thousand by 1870 and over 107,000 in 1880. Some people feared being overwhelmed by the Chinese and other Asians, and began passing laws against them. Anti-Chinese riots sprung up in some cities leading to the Chinese Exclusion Act (1882) which forbade Chinese immigration, overturning the Burlingame Treaty. Only a temporary ban at first, it became permanent in 1904. The Immigration Act of 1924 reduced the number of immigration visas and allocated them on the basis of national origin. The result was a reduction in the total number of immigrants. The Magnuson Act of 1943 repealed the Chinese Exclusion Acts. The Immigration and Nationality Act (McCarran-Walter Act) of 1952 made all people eligible for naturalization and increased the quota for Asians.

Contemporary Immigration

The Nationality Act Amendments of 1965 (the Hart-Cellar Act) abolished the system of national-origin quotas. It also officially abolished the restrictions on Asian immigration. This has led to a change in immigration patterns as more people started emigrating from counties other than Europe, as noted in the listing of immigration totals.

FIGURE 5.1	IMMIGRATION TOTALS
Continent/Country of Origin	**Number of Immigrants (1971–2002)**
Africa	825,700
Asia	7,331,500
Bangladesh	93,900
Cambodia	150,900
China	1,179,300
India	1,005,100
Japan	177,600
Laos	215,800
Philippines	1,508,100
South Korea	839,600
Vietnam	1,098,000
Europe	3,300,400
North America	9,844,500
Caribbean	2,936,800
Central America	1,334,200
Mexico	5,141,600
South America	1,479,700

Early immigration patterns to the United States saw poor people coming with the hope of a better life. While this continues to be a major motive of immigrants arriving today, the technology boom in the 1990s altered the pattern somewhat. The need for high-skilled workers—engineers, computer technicians, programmers, and the like—lured people from India, Vietnam, and other countries to fill the job markets in California's Silicon Valley, Washington's Dulles Corridor, Seattle's Kirkland, and other high-tech hotbeds. Yet, for the most part, new immigrants are needy, with, on average, less formal education and wealth.

Throughout its history, the United States has been a magnet for people from around the world. The immigration patterns have changed from Europeans to Asians to South Americans, and the acceptance and rejection of new arrivals has had its ups and downs. For now, the United States remains open to immigration, and the flow of people, legal and illegal, does not appear to be abating. Slightly over one million immigrants enter the United States each year, or about 125,000 per month. Such a large number of new immigrants presents challenges and opportunities for churches in the United States.

A STORY OF TWO CHURCHES

As people came to the New World and eventually the United States, they naturally brought their faith and churches with them. The early Dutch Reformed Church, being the oldest continually operating denomination in the United States, is one example.

Birthed out of the Protestant Reformation during the 1550s, the Reformed Church in America (RCA) traces its roots to the Dutch Reformed Church in the Netherlands. However, the Dutch did not come to the New World for religious liberty, but for commerce. When the Dutch East India Company founded New Amsterdam (modern-day Manhattan, New York) in 1609, no plan was made for establishing a church. As the small colony developed, the Dutch families requested that a church be established for them. Author Howard Hagemen describes the founding of the first Dutch church as follows: "In 1628 Domine Jonas Michaelius arrived in New Amsterdam, the first minister of the Reformed Church to set foot on these shores. Sometime in April of that year, in a loft over a mill, he celebrated the Lord's Supper and organized the congregation."[3]

As might be expected, the church focused almost exclusively on serving Dutch families. Little or no evangelistic effort was made to win the local Native Americans to Christ, and the church grew through the children of its members and some immigration of new Dutch families. By the 1650s, the town of New Amsterdam was essentially the same as at its founding.

Things began to change when England declared war on Holland in 1652. The English took over the city in 1664, and New Amsterdam became New York, while Fort Amsterdam was named Fort James in honor of James the Duke of York. The remaining Dutch church lacked a strong missionary drive, and the strong attachment to the Dutch language and the old ways slowed assimilation into the new culture of the developing new world.

Following the independence of the United States, the Dutch church established new churches by following its own sons and daughters as they joined the migration westward. However, reluctance to be Americanized stopped the church from participating in the religious revivals that spread across the western frontier. Over the years, Dutch migration patterns found the church being established primarily in the East and Midwest parts of the United States. Attempts to plant churches among people of other nationalities were not fruitful. Finally, in a gesture to Americanization, the denomination changed its name in 1867 from the Reformed Protestant Dutch Church to the Reformed Church in America.

While it was unstated, the denomination's mission was simply to serve the spiritual needs of Dutch people and their descendants. In some areas of the United States, this fact was reflected in the adage "If you ain't Dutch, you ain't much." It took over two hundred years for the denomination to establish churches in Kentucky (1909), Alabama (1911), California (1923), and Florida (1955). In spite of its inward focus and slow effort to plant churches, the denomination grew for nearly three hundred years, but primarily by reaching Dutch people.

From the swarms of Dutch immigrants that came to the United States during its three hundred plus years of history, the Reformed Church in America established strong and vibrant churches. Even with a denominational emphasis on social justice, especially among churches in the East in the 1960s and 1970s, few if any were multi-ethnic. The growth of Robert H. Schuller's Garden Grove Community Church (now the Crystal Cathedral) in the second half of the last century provided a model for outreach that was adopted by some churches in the denomination. Fresh church planting initiatives that arose out of California offered new ways to reach people for Christ, even those who were not Dutch. Slowly some denominational leaders and pastors began to wake up to the opportunities of reaching beyond their traditional target audience to other people in the United States. Despite some criticisms in the 1970s, the denomination did manage to fund several church planting initiatives and establish thirty-two churches in locations that were not familiar with Reformed churches.

As the twenty-first century dawned, some churches within the RCA started the transition toward multi-ethnicity. A prime example is Emmanuel Reformed Church in Paramount, California, mentioned already in chapter 2. During the first decade of the 2000s it has become a model for churches wishing to transition from a traditional, mono-ethnic white-culture ministry toward a diverse congregation composed of the descendants of white, Dutch, dairy farmers, African-Americans, and more recently arrived Latino families.

The Evangelical Free Church of America traces its roots in the United States to the late 1880s, when the Swedish Evangelical Free Mission in Boone, Iowa, was founded in October 1884. In 1950 this Swedish body merged with the Norwegian-Danish Evangelical Free Church Association to form a new denomination with 275 congregations. Since that time, the Evangelical Free Church has grown to include 1,321 churches in the United States.

Similar to the Dutch Reformed Church, the early Swedish, Norwegian, and Danish congregations grew primarily by reaching their own children and through church extension as members relocated throughout the United States. The seed for an emphasis on multi-ethnic churches was planted in the mid-1980s, as denominational leaders took note of the changing demographics in the United States. During the mid-1990s, a think tank of fifty church leaders met to pray, think, and envision the denomination's future. Out of that gathering a new mission statement was birthed which says, "We exist to glorify God by multiplying healthy churches among all people." This mission statement has served to direct the denomination for nearly two decades.

Toward the middle of the 2000s, it became clear that the denomination needed to put a face on its vision. In January 2004, the position of director of African-American ministries was established to serve as a bridge for existing and emerging black leaders in the denomination. This was followed by the addition of a director of Hispanic ministries and an executive director of reconciliation. More recently, an Asian pastor was added to the national board.

The Evangelical Free Church in America (EFCA) is an example of a denomination that has put emphasis, energy, and money on developing its multi-ethnic vision. The "all peoples" of the EFCA mission statement "encompasses every aspect of our lives: our skin color, our gender, our physical abilities and inabilities, even our economic station in life."[4] One of the denomination's church planting goals is that at least 20 percent of new churches will be either ethnic or multi-ethnic.

So how is the EFCA doing in its journey toward becoming multi-ethnic? A recent listing of churches shows that 15 percent of the 1,321 churches are either ethnic or multi-ethnic. Thus, it appears that the denomination is on its ways to being 20 percent non-Caucasian. A total of 9 percent of the churches are listed as multi-ethnic, 2 percent Asian, 2 percent Hispanic, and 1 percent African-American. Less than 1 percent of EFCA churches are comprised of other ethnic peoples.

These short case studies illustrate the typical progress of churches in the United States. Throughout most of US history, churches served the spiritual needs of people who emigrated from a particular country. Quite naturally these churches were mono-ethnic rather than multi-ethnic. For most of North America's older churches, as well as those of recent immigrants such as Koreans, Hmongs, Vietnamese, and others, the churches were and are targeted to specific ethnic peoples. Being first generation peoples, speaking a different language, feeling comfortable in a different culture, and other aspects made mono-ethnic churches the only real option. Only slowly have most churches and denominations made a move toward developing multi-ethnic churches in the United States.

Yet in spite of the current interest in transitioning mono-ethnic churches into multi-ethnic ones, or for that matter starting multi-ethnic churches from scratch, most people in the United States continue to be attracted to homogeneous churches that feature their language and cultural forms.

THE DIVERSITY MYTH

Driving around major cities or shopping in large malls gives us the impression that the United States is highly diverse; and it is in some places. Immigrants tend to enter the United States through key gateway cities, and most remain in those regions. Some immigrants are fanning out from major cities but the pace is relatively slow. For the most part, what we are seeing today is the development of micro melting pots, where the major locations of truly multi-ethnic populations are found primarily in California, Nevada, New Mexico, Arizona, east Texas, south Florida, and New York. Some areas of South Carolina, North Carolina, Arkansas, Georgia, Michigan, Minnesota, Wisconsin, Washington, Kansas, Utah, Rhode Island, New Jersey, Connecticut, and Pennsylvania are moving toward greater multi-ethnicity also. Most other states tend to remain primarily made up of one or perhaps two ethnic groups. In most counties of the United States, the presence of minority ethnic groups remains quite small. Only a handful of metropolitan areas are diverse enough to be considered true melting pots. This reality is sometimes described as "melting pot coagulation," referring to the fact that ethnic peoples tend to cluster in certain areas. For example, even with the growing diversity in the United States, one ethnic group dominates every county.

For this reason, multi-ethnic churches are normally found in metro areas where ethnic groups are pressed tightly together to the point that their sense of people consciousness (see next section) is broken down. Since the United States is not one large melting pot, where ethnic groups spread out and blend evenly from coast to coast, creating multi-ethnic churches will likely vary from region to region. Given the fact that people tend to cluster together in ethnic communities where they can be majority minorities, the planting of mono-ethnic churches will likely continue to be the primary form of church rather than multi-ethnic ones.

PEOPLE CONSCIOUSNESS

One of the major determining factors as to whether people will connect with a multi-ethnic church is the level of people consciousness—the degree that people think of themselves as uniquely different from others. Missiologist Tetsunao Yamamori calls this "ethnic consciousness" and defines it "as the intensity of awareness of one's distinct peoplehood based on [ethnicity], religion, and/or national origin."[5] The degree of people consciousness, of course, varies from one group to another and one person to another. All individuals and groups of people can be placed on a People Consciousness Scale.

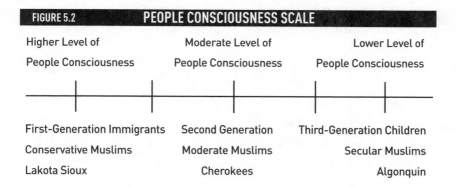

FIGURE 5.2   **PEOPLE CONSCIOUSNESS SCALE**

Higher Level of People Consciousness	Moderate Level of People Consciousness	Lower Level of People Consciousness
First-Generation Immigrants	Second Generation	Third-Generation Children
Conservative Muslims	Moderate Muslims	Secular Muslims
Lakota Sioux	Cherokees	Algonquin

One example of people consciousness is observed among first-generation ethnics such as Koreans, Columbians, or Nigerians. Each group usually evidences a high level of people consciousness that causes them to cluster in neighborhoods for support, safety, and encouragement. Thus, first-generation immigrants are usually found more to the left, while their third-generation children are further to the right. People consciousness normally declines as each succeeding generation assimilates more completely into the dominant culture of the adopted homeland. On the other hand, some groups, such as conservative Muslim Arabs, tend to maintain a strong people consciousness over several generations. They see themselves as Muslims first and members of a new culture last, a fact this is being observed in several European countries today. Subgroups of Native Americans are found in different places on the People Consciousness Scale. Lakota Sioux are often on the left, while Cherokees may be found in the middle, with Algonquin peoples totally to the right.

People consciousness provides for social cohesion among groups and individuals. In cultures that are strongly collective, that is, group oriented, the feeling of people consciousness is very strong. In such cultural contexts, the degree of people consciousness plays a major role in determining who may be married to whom, what business one pursues, and what religion is acceptable. Some countries and peoples demonstrate high people consciousness. For example, India, Japan, and Indonesia are comprised of people groups with high levels of people consciousness. Many individualistic cultures like the United States and most other Western societies have a lower people consciousness.

REACHING ETHNIC AMERICA

Given our mandate to make disciples of all the nations, churches throughout the United States must prioritize evangelism and outreach to the peoples in their communities whether it uses a mono- or multi-ethnic church approach. But how can we determine which approach will be the most effective with a particular people group? Tetsunao Yamamori suggested a workable approach three decades ago that we have adapted for our current situation in the United States.[6]

We suggest there are three basic approaches: assimilationist, identificational, and indigenous. The assimilationist approach affirms the traditional method of integrating ethnic peoples with low levels of people consciousness into churches of a dominant culture. The identificational approach affirms the effort to create multi-ethnic churches of shared governance, worship, and ministry with people of moderate people consciousness. The indigenous approach affirms the mono-ethnic approach that serves the needs of those with a high level of people consciousness. To obtain a snapshot of which groups in a given church community are most open to one of these three approaches, consider the following indices (figure 5.3). Select the number that most closely reflects the people group in your community.

	FIGURE 5.3	YAMAMORI SCALE	
High cultural adaptability	7 — 6 — 5 — 4 — 3 — 2 — 1	Low cultural adaptability
An establishment mentality "I'm here to stay"	7 — 6 — 5 — 4 — 3 — 2 — 1	A sojourner mentality "I plan to go home"
High aspiration to assimilate	7 — 6 — 5 — 4 — 3 — 2 — 1	Low aspiration to assimilate
Weak native religious identity	7 — 6 — 5 — 4 — 3 — 2 — 1	Strong native religious identity
Loss of contact with the community of one's kind	7 — 6 — 5 — 4 — 3 — 2 — 1	Contact with the community of one's kind.
Nonexistence of culturally bonded social organizations (clubs, associations)	7 — 6 — 5 — 4 — 3 — 2 — 1	Existence of culturally bonded social community centers, organizations
Nonexistence of culturally bonded mass media (non-English newspapers, radio, TV)	7 — 6 — 5 — 4 — 3 — 2 — 1	Existence of culturally bonded mass media
Lesser social distance (attitude)	7 — 6 — 5 — 4 — 3 — 2 — 1	Greater social distance (attitude)
Disappearance of racial discrimination (behavioral)	7 — 6 — 5 — 4 — 3 — 2 — 1	Persistence of racial discrimination (behavioral)
Lack of pride in national heritage	7 — 6 — 5 — 4 — 3 — 2 — 1	Pride in national heritage
Lighter skin	7 — 6 — 5 — 4 — 3 — 2 — 1	Darker skin
Area with high degree of ethnic mixing	7 — 6 — 5 — 4 — 3 — 2 — 1	Area with low degree of ethnic mixing
Exogamous marriages common	7 — 6 — 5 — 4 — 3 — 2 — 1	Endogamous marriages common
Second or later generations	7 — 6 — 5 — 4 — 3 — 2 — 1	First generation (immigrants)
Frequent change in last name	7 — 6 — 5 — 4 — 3 — 2 — 1	Pride in one's last name

continued

FIGURE 5.3	YAMAMORI SCALE continued	
Upward social mobility	7 — 6 — 5 — 4 — 3 — 2 — 1	Minimal upward social mobility
Dispersion of the people	7 — 6 — 5 — 4 — 3 — 2 — 1	Concentration of the people
Absence of "power movements"	7 — 6 — 5 — 4 — 3 — 2 — 1	Presence of "power movements"
Low consciousness of lineage	7 — 6 — 5 — 4 — 3 — 2 — 1	High consciousness of lineage
Community less than 15 percent ethnic	7 — 6 — 5 — 4 — 3 — 2 — 1	Community over 50 percent ethnic

The most fruitful way to reach people who register between 20 and 40 points on the Yamamori scale is likely through the indigenous approach. The high level of people consciousness within this group means that a mono-ethnic church and ministry is appropriate. However, if a people scores between 120 and 140 points, they most often will be reached through an assimilationist approach. It is the people group that falls in the middle range, say 60 to 100 points, that is the best candidate for the identificational approach—a multi-ethnic church.

FIGURE 5.4		
Lower Level of People Consciousness Use the Assimilationist Approach (120–140 points)	Moderate Level of People Consciousness Use the Identificational Approach (60–100 points)	Higher Level of People Consciousness Use the Indigenous Approach (20–40 points)

As a prime example, consider recent Latino immigrants located in southern California. A significant number of this people group continues to have a high level of people consciousness. Due to the close proximity of Mexico to California, many Latinos show evidence of a sojourner mentality, a low aspiration to assimilate into the predominant culture and a high commitment to their native religious (Roman Catholic) identity. They reside in a community nearing 50 percent saturation of their own kind, and there is a large number of culturally bounded social organizations and mass media. In many cases there is minimal social upward mobility, while at the same time there is a strong sense of pride in one's name and national identity. For this particular people group, it will usually take a mono-ethnic church to reach them for Christ (indigenous approach). However, some models of multi-ethnic churches may also be able to reach them.

The important insight for our discussion is to understand that multi-ethnic churches are most likely to be found in societies with low people consciousness. The level of people consciousness is an indicator of how willing people are to gather in multi-ethnic churches. Throughout the years, as individuals or families with a high people consciousness live in a highly individualistic country or society, inevitably there will be change in the individual and social context that breaks down people consciousness. As societies become filled with members who have a lower people consciousness, they tend to group together around other homogeneous characteristics. What allows for multi-ethnic churches to be formed today is the great bringing together of people, societies, and cultures into close proximity in the urban centers of the world. The pressure of the urban world tends to break down people consciousness, which allows for people to gather together around other characteristics. The latter situation is true of many people in the United States today, especially those located in urban centers.

PUTTING INSIGHTS TO WORK

1. Reflect on your own church and/or denomination. How does the history of immigration in the United States correspond to your own church's history? What impact does it have on your church or denomination today?

2. What groups of people in your community appear to have a high level of people consciousness? Which ones are moderate? Which groups show evidence of lower people consciousness?

3. Does your community appear to be one where a multi-ethnic church could be started? If so, how do you know?

PATTERNS OF MULTI-ETHNIC CHURCHES

The worship pastor must always be of a different ethnicity than the senior pastor.
—Pastor Jay Pankratz

On the journey to become a multi-ethnic church, which in its fullest form is an elusive goal for most churches, a number of steps or patterns are observed that create the space for other cultural expressions. For instance, sharing the church facilities with another cultural group is often a beginning step. Worshiping together in occasional, combined services is another small step. In this chapter we examine the patterns of ministry that multi-ethnic churches follow in the areas of worship, evangelism, discipleship, conflict resolution, and church government. In the most practical outworking of the dynamics of multi-ethnic churches, these are the areas in which the unique features of ministry are demonstrated.

WORSHIP PATTERNS

When multiple ethnicities first come together in a church's worship services, many churches begin to consciously identify themselves as multi-ethnic. Accommodation or adaptation of the worship music and style mark most congregations' first observable steps on the way to being multi-ethnic. As time goes on, other significant changes follow if a church is able to manage the redefinition of identity that such changes inevitably force.

In modifying the worship forms and styles, multi-ethnic churches adopt various forms. Some serve the diversity of the body by starting separate worship services based on language. First Baptist Church of Flushing, New York, conducts worship services in four languages—English, Spanish, Mandarin, and Cantonese—under one senior pastor, who happens to be Chinese.[1] The English and Spanish services have their own pastor while one associate pastor serves both the Cantonese and Mandarin attendees. Each pastor preaches in his own congregation, but occasionally they rotate pulpits to have exposure to the other congregations to whom they collectively minister. Upon first glance this form seems to separate groups into separate homogeneous units, which to some degree is correct. Closer examination, however, reveals that each language group actually serves a multi-ethnic population that has language as a common denominator. The Spanish language service, for example, brings together a number of Latino nationalities and cultures. Each language service seeks to reduce social and cultural differences by utilizing a musical style, worship form (kneeling, dancing, swaying), and order of worship that fits the congregation in question. Ethnicities other than those targeted are welcome to attend these non-English speaking services but most choose to attend the English language service.

Other multi-ethnic churches do not try to operate different language services, choosing to hold worship services only in English. When this happens, several motivations and patterns are usually observed. Some churches simply do not try to accommodate other ethnicities by modifying their worship style, believing that their diverse congregation rallies around another common denominator other than ethnic background. Saddleback Church in southern California serves a predominantly Caucasian audience but empowers diversity by hosting multiple worship styles in different venues on its church campus, most, if not all, in English.[2] Redeemer Presbyterian in New York City, for example, holds morning worship services using a classical, Anglo-oriented, Presbyterian liturgy, and evening services using a jazz worship style. Among their attendees, however, is a large Asian population as well as Anglos, Latinos, and African-Americans. The great majority are highly educated, upwardly mobile, and mostly singles in their twenties and thirties. While a person's particular ethnicity seems to be less of an issue than life stage and education, most would argue that Redeemer is multi-ethnic.

Another pattern of English-only services in a multi-ethnic church are those churches that attempt to blend in one service the worship forms that serve a variety of cultural tastes and perspectives. A decision to attempt blending is often driven by a desire to keep everyone together, thus keeping multi-ethnicity prominently displayed as a statement to the community. Churches that emphasize racial reconciliation or wish to represent in a single worship service the diversity found in their local neighborhood (see the discussion in chapter 10) may prefer this model. Sunrise Church in Rialto, California, does this with its main English services (though it also operates a service in Spanish). By deliberately mixing Anglo, Latino, gospel music, as well as urban and contemporary worship forms together into one service, the church communicates something of relevance for everyone. Through this blending, it teaches an appreciation for other ways of praising God.

Sometimes the decision to blend cultural forms into a single English language service is made out of necessity due to the lack of space or leadership to operate independent language services. In these cases, blending styles in a single worship service is the best that can be done until more space becomes available or new leaders are identified. Sometimes what is done out of necessity becomes ingrained into the theology and personality of the church, and is therefore retained for different reasons over time. In any event, English language services are the most frequently blended services in North American multi-ethnic churches.

In blending services to make them suitable for serving diverse members of the congregation, some churches prefer to develop separate choirs, worship teams, and/or worship leaders. Each contributes to part of every service, or worship styles may rotate, featuring a particular style periodically through the month. In both cases, the potential for broadening the cultural horizons of those who attend is great. Larger congregations, however, usually handle the complexity of these arrangements best with a worship leader who has a great ability to move between the different styles with ease.

Other congregations, such as First Baptist Church in the Wilshire District of Los Angeles, blend their worship styles by conducting bilingual or multilingual services with the help of a translator. In this church, hymnals are available in three languages, and singing is done in one's own language in what is largely a traditional Anglo worship style.[3] Over time, however, this pattern produces fatigue both for the congregation and worship leaders.

EVANGELISM PATTERNS

It was primarily with evangelism in mind that Donald McGavran first articulated the Homogeneous Unit Principle (HUP). Observing that people prefer not to cross cultural barriers in order to understand and accept the gospel, he concluded that we should do everything possible to eliminate the foreign packaging that we as cross-cultural workers unconsciously add to it. That is to say, we often expect people to understand the gospel and respond to it in the same way that we do as Westerners. But when we do that, we mix North American values with the essential gospel message. For that reason, the goal is to see the gospel become indigenous to the people we are communicating it to as soon as possible. The Christian message naturally causes offense because it confronts sin. But we need to make sure that the offense we bring is due to the essential challenge of the gospel message and not the cultural wrapping in which we carry it.

Unfortunately many zealous advocates of the multi-ethnic church see the Homogeneous Unit Principle as being the enemy of multi-ethnicity. Conceding its value for evangelism, they seek to confine it there. Mark DeYmaz and Harry Li state:

> The HUP is a valid strategy for evangelism, but a strategy misapplied to the local church. If the goal is to evangelize, then by all

means target a people group and provide them with the Word of God in their own language. Sing to them in a musical genre they understand and become incarnate in their culture so that the gospel is expressed through customs, mores, and traditions they readily embrace. But things change once you commit yourself to establishing a local church. You are no longer at liberty to create a congregation of exclusive worshipers—that's just not a biblical option.[4]

While we agree that exclusive mono-ethnic churches are not biblical (see chapter 3), we believe that inclusive mono-ethnic churches are biblical. What is the difference? Exclusive mono-ethnic churches shut out all those unlike themselves, and that type of mono-ethnic church is not biblical. On the other hand, inclusive mono-ethnic churches who welcome the stranger, the alien, and the foreigner into their fellowship are biblical even though they are centered around a single, dominant people group.

The problem with the position taken by DeYmaz and Li is that they attempt to separate evangelism from the church. Evangelism, they allow, can be done using a homogeneous approach, but once a person becomes a believer he or she must move into a heterogeneous, multi-ethnic fellowship. What seems more true to Scripture is that, as we grow in Christ, we should realize our responsibility as citizens of the heavenly kingdom and the implications of salvation that make us members of one family. We must, therefore, be more accepting and loving toward those different from us.

The truth is that both homogeneous and heterogeneous ministry forms can be used for evangelism depending on the audience to whom we are communicating. Using the Homogeneous Unit Principle for guidance, we can say that most people are more easily won to the gospel when they are approached in cultural forms that correspond to what is familiar to them. Practically speaking, when we use their language, music style, communication media, and cultural forms to reach them, we are more fruitful. If we first force them to enter a blended culture that requires them to cross cutural hurdles, we will put an unnecessary barrier in their way. The exception to this pattern is seen when a multi-ethnic church presents the gospel to a multi-ethnic community. In the plurality of the city, an outreach strategy that is carried out by a diverse community of believers who have experienced reconciliation can be a powerful testimony to the power of the gospel. The unity of the worshiping multi-ethnic congregation is also a means of testifying to mono-ethnic groups of a new relationship that is possible in Christ.

Despite the earlier quotation from DeYmaz and Li that isolates homogeneous evangelistic efforts away from the functioning of the church, they later refer to five models of outreach used by multi-ethnic churches that seem to blend homogeneous and heterogeneous models.[5] These include:

- An emphasis on first-generation (1.0) outreach: In this model, a multi-ethnic church establishes a mono-ethnic worship and outreach site to reach out to a new minority group that is currently underserved.
- An emphasis on world mission: This outreach seeks to use the immigrant communities' relationship networks in their homelands to establish new bodies of believers.
- An emphasis on local evangelism: In this case, a multi-ethnic church seeks to reach its own community by employing effective teaching pastors and worship styles from a variety of ethnicities that match the ethnic groups in the target area.
- An emphasis on racial reconciliation: By addressing the pain and racism that has divided communities in the past, these churches seek to build bridges to the unchurched community that has experienced division and racial strife.
- An emphasis on community engagement: Churches using this model seek to develop cross-cultural relationships with people in the urban context through incarnational approaches.

The value of these models is to show the variety of ways the multi-ethnic church engages the unchurched (although most of them use homogeneous approaches). If the evangelism method is matched to the composition of the target audience, both homogeneous and heterogeneous models can be effective.

DISCIPLESHIP PATTERNS

As a general rule, evangelism is more effective when the message is presented in forms that are most familiar to the hearer. Therefore, in most cases, homogeneous groups that match the hearer's culture are preferred. The exception to this rule, as we previously noted, occurs when the hearers are at home in a pluralistic, ethnically mixed context. In these cases, ethnically mixed (heterogeneous) outreach efforts may actually be more appealing than a mono-ethnic (homogeneous) approach. In either case, when people become Christians and are enfolded into a worshiping community, one of the discipleship goals is to teach them the importance of loving those unlike themselves. This form of selfless love was modeled by Jesus and held up as the path in which the believer must walk as empowered by the Spirit. In fact, a movement toward greater inclusiveness and acceptance of the other is an outcome of sanctification. Therefore, in the continuum presented in chapter 3, believers are called upon to grow in their acceptance of the other. In other words, greater tolerance of heterogeneity to recognize the intrinsic worth and beauty of all of God's people seems to be a measure of spiritual growth. To embark on this journey is what the strongest advocates for the multi-ethnic church are calling the church to do.

The goal of this vision then is to equip and structure the church so that multi-ethnicity is seen at every level of its existence—from the large worship service down to the smallest friendship circle. It approaches the ideal when diversity is in full harmony within itself. It is seen when believers of any ethnicity or cultural background are so invested in each other's lives—praying for each other, teaching each other, and serving each other—that ethnic, cultural, or generational distinctions are erased or at least become irrelevant. The ultimate test comes when parents are willing to give their sons and daughters to interethnic marriages with other strong believers in the church. But whether it goes to that point or not, the vision for the multi-ethnic church is to model unity in the midst of diversity, and to apply that to the discipleship functions of the church. So how does this play out in practice?

The truth of the matter is that most multi-ethnic churches employ both heterogeneous and homogeneous groupings throughout the church's ministry. Though the goal of most multi-ethnic churches is to model heterogeneity in all aspects of church life, the reality is that few churches, if any, ever achieve this level of multi-ethnic purity, even highly celebrated multi-ethnic churches. This reality is not unlike that which is seen in the cell church movement. Though the goal of many cell churches is to have 100 percent of their attendees involved in a cell group, it is a rare church that achieves more than 80 percent of its members being in cell groups. In the same manner, nearly all multi-ethnic churches have groupings within the church that are best described as homogeneous, mono-ethnic groups.

As a general rule, the larger the group the more likely it is heterogeneous. Large worship services are more likely to be multi-ethnic than small groups or Sunday school classes. Some churches do not attempt to drive multi-ethnicity down to the level of small groups. They are content to let the larger gatherings serve that purpose. In these churches, discipleship happens primarily in language- or culture-specific groups along homogeneous unit lines. Other churches eagerly encourage their people to mix with other ethnicities in small group Bible studies, classes, service ministries, and sports teams, for it is at this level that one really begins to appreciate the richness that the other group brings. Many people in multi-ethnic churches take advantage of these opportunities. This kind of interaction fosters a deeper appreciation and understanding across ethnic lines and is to be commended. In many cases, however, such groupings are more common in youth or children's ministries, or in the English-speaking congregations if services are held in more than one language. This pattern is largely due to the fact that it is in those ministries that most second generation immigrants are found and they are more likely to be withdrawing from the traditional culture orientation of their parents.

One beauty of the multi-ethnic church is that it has the freedom to sponsor both homogeneous and heterogeneous gatherings and allow their people to engage as they feel comfortable. Of course, encouragement is always given to step outside one's comfort zone and learn from brothers and sisters who are different from one's own group. But the multi-ethnic church that uses both types of ministry groups offers a special advantage to the immigrant family. In one church, both the first generation and the second generation can find places where each can grow and explore without being forced into one model or the other. Even when families split up to attend different kinds of gatherings (homogenous groups for the first generation and mixed groups for the second generation), they are still attending a single church with a common theology rather than being pulled toward two different churches where they have little interaction. The multi-ethnic church is uniquely equipped to serve the immigrant family at all stages of their family life cycle.

Before leaving this subject of discipleship patterns in multi-ethnic churches, it is useful to go back to the study undertaken by pastor Art Lucero of Sunrise Church in Rialto, California, which produced some surprising results. Working with Robert Weaver from Azusa-Pacific University, Lucero sought to answer the question of whether minority group members had a strong sense of belonging to a multi-ethnic church in which there was no ethnic majority?[6] To answer this question, they developed several hypotheses to test. They theorized, for example, that members of Sunrise Church who had been attending for a longer period would have a greater percentage of cross-racial friends in their closest friendship circles than people who had attended for a shorter period of time. They further believed that the multitude of opportunities for social interaction that the church provided would over time help people confront their own biases and prejudices and therefore be more likely to invite cross-racial friends into these close friendship circles. What they discovered was surprising. They discovered that those who had a long history in attending multi-ethnic churches and agreed with the vision of such churches were nevertheless largely homogeneous in their interactions with their closest friends. Although they had good friends among those of other ethnicities, they still grouped with people like themselves in their closest circles. Findings such as these do not negate the goals or activities of multi-ethnic churches. Those churches have made good progress. But it does demonstrate the difficulty of changing natural and well-established patterns of relationships and the difficulty of overcoming the power of culture. It also establishes the power of homogeneity working at the deepest levels of relationships.

CONFLICT RESOLUTION PATTERNS

Conflict is a natural by-product of bringing together people from diverse backgrounds and perspectives to work toward some common goal. Even for churches that are mono-ethnic, who theoretically share many assumptions and values, conflict is a frequent tool used by the Enemy—Satan. When diversity is increased, the potential for divisive conflict increases exponentially. Not only are numerous assumptions dramatically different between cultures; but the ways of resolving conflict vary between cultures as well. In many Asian cultures, for example, direct confrontation is almost never entertained, and, if it is displayed, it has already passed a crisis level. The values of saving face and showing respect to others almost always means that an intermediary is sought who can negotiate between parties to find a mutually agreeable solution. This process is indirect and time-consuming, requiring patience and fortitude. Naturally, this conflict resolution style is very different from that of many Westerners who are quite direct and forthright in their communication.

Certainly most multi-ethnic churches of any size have not only encountered more than their share of conflict, but they have learned patterns for engaging it constructively so that it builds toward greater understanding rather than tearing the church apart. More often than not, they see conflict as an opportunity to glorify God and build up the body to love and good deeds, not as something to be feared and avoided at all costs. Indeed, it has been said that most growing churches have evidence of conflict. If you find a church with no conflict, it is probably just a couple steps away from the grave. In the same manner, most multi-ethnic churches have learned patterns for surfacing conflict early and dealing with it in constructive ways that push people toward greater interdependence and mutuality. Senior pastors often display skills in facilitation and organizational alignment that help diverse groups talk to and work through issues. They work with their coleaders to build high trust between each other and also equip their staff to do the same. Moreover, they spend a considerable amount of time in shaping a shared vision that captures the best aspirations of each group. This vision, supported by good biblical preaching and teaching and illustrated in the activities of the church, is kept before the congregation as a reminder of the ultimate goals that it shares together. In these ways the multi-ethnic church has much to share with the larger body of Christ.

CHURCH GOVERNANCE PATTERNS

As a church's membership composition becomes more multi-ethnic, natural leaders from diverse ethnic and cultural backgrounds emerge. These leaders have credibility and respect from their natural relationship networks. They are thought leaders who encounter ideas and interpret them back to their friends and family, most of whom share their same ethnicity or are affiliated on the basis of some other common denominator (age, marital status, gender, education). As emerging opinion leaders, they are the ones to whom others take cues on how to respond to opportunities and threats to their acceptance and/or influence in the larger body. Their emergence as leaders is primarily related to their natural talents, personality, acquired skills, prior experience, spiritual gifts, and calling. Secondarily, they may emerge as leaders due to education, financial success, or prior positions of leadership. In any event, leaders of multi-ethnic churches need to continuously scan the congregation to identify these leaders early, and to begin recruiting, training, and deploying them into ministry roles as soon as possible.

Whether ministry leaders are attempting to transition a church to embrace a greater level of multi-ethnicity or simply trying to equip the leadership team to manage the more complex dynamics of a multi-ethnic church, it is critical that they find and recruit leaders who can put the ministry vision and goals into the language of their followers in ways that make sense to them. To achieve the full potential of the multi-ethnic church, each segment of the church needs to be valued, enlisted, and mobilized to achieve the larger purposes before them.

Likewise, two key organizational development tasks must be carried out in tandem if the church is to achieve its purpose. The first of these tasks is empowerment. That is, ministry leaders must be able to provide the resources for each group to prosper. Those resources may relate to ministry funds, space for meetings, or representation on leadership teams. Leaders also need to remove the barriers that prevent the various segments of the church from being effective, whether they are communication barriers, organizational barriers, or something else.

The second key organizational development task is that of alignment. This task is especially critical in multi-ethnic churches where no single cultural construct is there to guide decision-making and action. Due to the complexity of managing a multi-ethnic church with the various perspectives and worldviews competing for attention, the alignment around a compelling vision and a set of core values is essential. Here is where the use of tribal leaders (opinion leaders for a specific group), who can go back to their constituencies and articulate the shared vision to their followers is vitally important. Yet this task is often neglected, resulting in segments of the multi-ethnic congregation not owning the direction and decisions of the leadership. Even more important, if the task of empowerment described earlier is engaged without a corresponding effort to align the diverse elements of the congregation, the church will move to a point of gridlock where newly empowered people work at cross-purposes with each other. When this happens, the level of conflict rises, and the stability of the multi-ethnic church is threatened. Misunderstandings and hurt feelings can take months to heal. So identifying, recruiting, training, deploying, empowering, and aligning leaders of the various segments of the church is essential to take the church to a greater level of multi-ethnic integration.

As lay leaders representing multiple ethnicities and other kinds of congregational diversity are identified and honored, a powerful message is sent to the congregation at large as to the values and direction of the congregation. Representatives among the leadership that "look like us" give some assurance that everyone's voice is heard and the concerns and needs of each group are considered. In Acts 6, the early church dealt with this problem in a straightforward fashion by appointing deacons with Greek-sounding names to supervise the daily distribution of food for Grecian widows. Virtually all successful multi-ethnic churches display a wide diversity among their lay leaders, from small group leaders to worship leaders to elders, deacons, and governing board members.

As they grow in size and add more staff, many multi-ethnic churches raise their professional staff from within. Competent leaders representing minority groups who have also proven themselves to be of godly character and effective in ministry are appointed to paid staff positions, thus increasing their visibility and influence.

Staffing strategies for pastoral positions vary between multi-ethnic churches. Some churches seek to compose their pastoral leadership teams in ways that reflect the relative composition of the congregation. Using this staffing philosophy, if 30 percent of the congregation is of Asian descent, then roughly 30 percent of the professional and lay leadership should also be Asian, assuming there are sufficient numbers of spiritually qualified candidates. Still other churches, after studying the population trends of their neighborhood and the membership composition of their congregation, may choose to staff in order to reach an underrepresented ethnic group or demographic segment in the neighborhood. For example, if population trends in the neighborhood show that in the next ten years a large number of Latinos will likely be moving into the area, a multi-ethnic church may choose to hire a Latin-American pastor to develop ministries to reach them even if there are currently few Latinos attending the church. Staffing decisions can do much to steer a church toward a more multi-ethnic composition and therefore should be engaged in much dialogue with current leadership.

Harold Korver came to Emmanuel Reformed Church in Paramount, California, in 1971 on the precondition that the church be willing to embark on a journey to become more missional and relevant to the community. Formerly a dairy farming area in the greater Los Angeles metropolitan area, by the 1980s Paramount was experiencing a significant transition in ethnic composition. Latinos and African-Americans were moving in and the whites were moving out. Faced with the choice to move the church out of the area to follow its members, or stay and minister in the context where it was planted, Harold Korver led his congregation to take a step of faith and stay. In doing so, the church made a decision to become more multi-ethnic and reach out to its new neighbors. When Ken Korver succeeded his father as senior pastor of the church, he continued this vision by hiring three Latinos and one African-American on the ministry staff. These staffing decisions sent strong signals to the congregation and community—this church would be a place where everyone was welcome and each culture could find a home.

Similar stories are repeated in other multi-ethnic churches such as First Baptist Church in Flushing, New York, mentioned earlier in this chapter. Three Chinese pastors serve on its ministry staff, along with an Anglo pastor, a Latino pastor, and an Indian youth minister. Sunrise Church in Rialto, California has a highly diverse ministry team composed of Latinos, Anglos, African-Americans, and a Guatemalan, among others. The diversity of these leadership teams shows a high level of integration within the body.

How these teams function differs from church to church. At Emmanuel Reformed, the pastors share the ministry responsibilities for the whole congregation, taking turns to preach or lead worship without regard to ethnicity, though two of them give particularized focus to the Latino service where Spanish language fluency is essential. These ministry leaders work seamlessly together as a cohesive leadership team.

In the case of First Baptist Church in Flushing, most pastors are assigned to a specific language congregation, each of which has its own Coworker Council that provides the care for each congregation. At least one representative from each of the three congregations sits on the governing board that addresses issues of common concern under the direction of Henry Kwan, the senior pastor. The three congregations share a common children's and youth ministry to effectively serve second-generation members. On special occasions, the three congregations come together for joint services supported by trilingual or quadra-lingual translation.

The leadership structures of most organizations usually represent the point of greatest vulnerability, the church included. The leadership of the church has the greatest power to shape the corporate culture and the identity of the congregation. The leaders are the ones who must remind the flock of God's purposes, identify and communicate the core values they will live by, and give definition to the vision. If the leaders are not united or clear on direction for the future, confusing messages are sent to the followers, or worse yet, conflict can erupt. If the diverse leaders who make up the multi-ethnic church begin to polarize, the negative impact can be multiplied through the ranks. High trust must be built between leaders so that they act as one and model to the rest of the congregation the unity that is to characterize the family of God.

Probably the most difficult level of multicultural engagement is that of leadership style. It is much easier to form multi-ethnic outreach activities, worship services, or discipleship groups than to fundamentally reshape the leadership around a multi-ethnic, multicultural identity. In terms of the organization, it is perhaps at this point that the implicit assumptions that form the foundation for worldview are most difficult to confront. It is one thing to hire a diverse staff that represents the composition of the church or community, but it is a far more difficult challenge to construct a decision-making style that honors the traditions of each contributing culture. Even for churches that wish to be thoroughly multicultural, this may be the most difficult challenge.

How decisions will be made is a key question every diverse leadership team must determine. Will decisions be made in an Asian style that defers the decision to the oldest person in the room? Or will the team follow an Eastern European style that has long been dictated by those leaders in positional power? Will all decisions be made by consensus? Or will leaders follow a Western democratic style where everyone gets an equal voice and the final decision is made through voting? At the end of the day, a single model of decision-making must be adopted. Every tradition cannot be honored simultaneously; otherwise nothing will get done efficiently. It is at this point that some evidence of the most dominant culture will prevail.

Every leadership style has embedded in it assumptions and values that are shaped by a particular culture.

Perhaps the ultimate reality is that everything in the multi-ethnic church will not necessarily be equal, proportional to the size of the groups that make it up, or even fair. Some group will always be at a certain disadvantage or will have to yield to another group or a higher good. But as each group learns to be sensitive and loving to the other, willing to submit to and serve and honor the other, it will display the mind of Christ and reflect the grace that Christ showed toward the church.

In the end, the goal of constructing a multi-ethnic church in every aspect of organizational life may prove to be an elusive goal, an ideal construct. A church that reaches this point of multi-ethnic integration, however, has truly achieved a great thing nevertheless.

PUTTING INSIGHTS TO WORK

1. Describe the issues your church has faced with worship, evangelism, discipleship, conflict resolution, and church government.

2. If you are in a multi-ethnic church, which of the patterns described in this chapter have been the most challenging to you? How have you dealt with some of the issues?

3. How does your church make decisions in a multi-ethnic context? Which cultural model of decision-making tends to dominate? How does this work in your context?

7
MONO-ETHNIC CHURCHES

Birds of a feather flock together.
—ancient proverb

Walk into most churches and look around. What do you see? What do you look for at first glance? If you are like most people, you look to see if there are other people like yourself in the congregation. Are you young? Then you hope to see some young faces. If you are older you expect to see folks with grey hair. Do you have a family? If so, you no doubt wish to find some other families with children about the age of your own.

It is a natural fact of life that people tend to gather with others who have similar backgrounds, interests, and kinship. As the old proverb declares, "Birds of a feather flock together." Anyone who takes the time to observe birds knows this proverb is literally true. Pigeons gather in city parks, geese fly south in flocks, and crows swarm to protect their young. The proverb is also applicable to human relationships. One of the earliest known citations of the proverb dates back to Benjamin Jowett's 1856 translation of Plato's *Republic*. He translates Plato as saying, "Men of my age flock together; we are birds of a feather, as the old proverb says."[1] Evidently even Plato was aware of this proverb, or one very similar to it, as early as 380 B.C.

This principle, which we all practice in one form or another, has come to be called the Homogeneous Unit Principle in missiology circles. While it is just one of many principles that help churches grow by making disciples of all the nations, it has become the most controversial and most misunderstood. Even though the inclination or bent of humans to connect in affinity groups has been observed and acknowledged throughout history, for some reason when this practice is observed in churches, it is often declared to be wrong. Critics point out that (1) since the church is to be one; (2) since the barrier between Jews and Greeks has been broken down; (3) since Christ broke down the middle wall of hostility; and (4) since the eschatological church is described as worshiping together, biblical churches must be heterogeneous. In other words, homogeneity (affinity) in the church is wrong.

The unseen thread flowing through most of the criticisms is a misunderstanding of a homogeneous unit and the Homogeneous Unit Principle. Misunderstandings, of course, span a large gap from mild to extreme. Some see homogeneous units as artificially erected groups forced upon the church.[2] Others criticize homogeneous units as being perpetuated by sinful, or at least misguided, people.[3] One mild misunderstanding sees homogeneity through the narrow lens of church attendance, such as, "People want to go to church with people who are basically like them."[4] A more extreme misunderstanding views a homogeneous unit as perpetuating racism. For instance, one critic writes, "The homogeneous unit principle allowed the white church to further propagate a system of white privilege by creating a system of de facto segregation."[5]

From our perspective, all these criticisms are highly unfortunate. For the most part, they perpetuate confusion of the issue and in some extreme cases, they come close to slandering honest Christians who are seeking to fulfill their calling in Christ. In truth, the homogeneous unit is not narrowly focused on church attendance, nor is it promoting any system of racism. It is not an artificially created idea from the minds of misguided social theorists. Critics who espouse such views have not done their homework and clearly illustrate a surface understanding of missiological theory while creating ongoing confusion about what a homogeneous unit describes. Homogeneous units actually arise from human instincts that developed in a social construct created by God. That homogeneous units, and the Homogeneous Unit Principle, have been misused by humans at certain times and places does not negate the reality that they are a construct of creation. Retired missionary and professor Walther Olsen declares, "What gravity is to the physical realm, the HUP [Homogeneous Unit Principle] is to the socio-cultural realm."[6]

WHAT IS A HOMOGENEOUS UNIT?

If you are a football fan, you most likely know of the legendary coach of the Green Bay Packers, Vince Lombardi. After taking over as coach of this storied franchise, he became frustrated with the ineffective practice and play of the team. As the story goes (we cannot confirm it is factual, but it is a great one), he called the team together, picked up a football, and said something like, "Gentlemen. This is a football." In a similar vein, let us start at the beginning by defining and describing a homogeneous unit.

Missiologist Donald McGavran articulated the Homogeneous Unit Principle in 1971. The principle was implicit in his earlier works, such as *The Bridges of God* (1955) and *How Churches Grow* (1959), but his mature statement came in *Understanding Church Growth* (1971). In that book he said, "A homogeneous unit is simply a section of society in which all the members have some characteristic in common."[7] As one can observe, this definition of the homogeneous unit makes no direct reference to race, ethnicity, or church attendance, although it can be applied to each one in certain contexts. A homogeneous unit is present whenever members of society gather in groups where clear characteristics are observable, and where the characteristics form a sort of glue that binds the group together. For example, a women's Bible study is a homogeneous unit because it is comprised of women. A youth baseball team is a homogeneous unit because it is a gathering of young baseball players. A VFW (Veterans of Foreign Wars) post's social event is homogeneous because it is a meeting of proud military people. Each of these examples is a homogeneous unit, but in none is the common characteristic race or ethnicity. So the first important thing to understand about homogeneity is that it is not about racial segregation or the placing of one ethnic group above another.

A second important understanding is that all groups normally include homogeneity and heterogeneity, unity and diversity. Building on the examples above, a women's Bible study is homogeneous because it is comprised of females, but it may also be heterogeneous if the women are of different ethnic, economic, and educational backgrounds. A youth baseball team is homogeneous since the members are all baseball players, but heterogeneous if the players are boys and girls. A VFW social event is homogeneous due to everyone's connection to veterans of foreign wars, but heterogeneous if members are men and women, college graduates and high school graduates, blue-collar and white-collar. The existence of homogeneity and heterogeneity in such groups is illustrated in the following table.

FIGURE 7.1

Group	Homogeneity	Heterogeneity
Women's Bible study	All females	Different ethnic, economic, and educational backgrounds
Youth baseball team	All baseball players	Girls and boys
VFW post	All veterans of foreign wars with their families, and friends	Men, women, college graduates, high school graduates, blue-collar workers, white-collar workers, etc.

The bottom line is that all groups are homogeneous and heterogeneous at the same time. In fact it is nearly impossible to be solely homogeneous. Unity and diversity run side by side. Diversity allows for people of various cultures to worship as they desire, but from time to time come together in a function of unity.

A third insight about homogeneous units often missed is that the common characteristic may be a worldview, perspective, or attitude. The glue that binds people together might be a particular political perspective, theological viewpoint, or passionate commitment. For instance, it is common to list churches as evangelistic churches, teaching churches, or social-action churches. Classifying churches in this manner uses the common passion that binds the people together. Thus, when churches are formed around a common passion of demonstrating the oneness of people from different ethnic groups, economic groups, or social strata, they can be considered homogeneous. Churches that are multi-ethnic are homogeneous! Multi-ethnicity becomes their homogeneity.

As these few illustrations demonstrate, "the homogeneous unit is an elastic concept, its meaning depending on the context in which it is used." It can be a political unit or subunit, "a segment of society whose common characteristic is a culture or a language," a family and clan, or a host of other units defined by geography, lineage, dialect, or a number of other characteristics.[8]

As discussed in chapter 5, the level of people consciousness is a strong indicator of homogeneity or heterogeneity. This is particularly true with immigrants, but people consciousness also exists, for example, among members of a youth baseball team that has a strong team identity. If, however, there is no strong identity among members of a team, it is not a true homogeneous unit, since each player sees him- or herself as separate from the team. Thus, if the people attending a church have a strong people consciousness as members of that particular church, it is a homogeneous unit no matter how diverse the group is according to other criteria.

WHAT IS THE HOMOGENEOUS UNIT PRINCIPLE?

With this basic understanding of a homogeneous unit in place, missiologist Donald McGavran articulated the following principle: "People like to become Christians without crossing racial, linguistic, or class barriers."[9] Note first that this is a principle of evangelism rather than fellowship.

McGavran was not discussing how to get people to fellowship together, but how to win the most people to faith in Christ. It is a principle of inclusion, not exclusion. The Homogeneous Unit Principle focuses on how we can bring more people into the church, not, as some extremists would postulate, a way to keep people out of the church.[10] Critics tend to confuse the beginning of discipleship with the ending of discipleship. Belief and introduction to a local church is the first step. As new believers are empowered by the Holy Spirit, they begin a lifelong journey of spiritual growth that leads them to love God and their neighbors as themselves. Without the indwelling Holy Spirit, unbelievers do not have the inherent power to love God with all their hearts or their neighbors as themselves. The first and second commandments are important in spiritual growth, but salvation must come first.

When McGavran introduced the Homogeneous Unit Principle, he was answering the question of whether a person can become a Christian without changing his or her family of origin, ethnic identity, or clan. McGavran had faced this challenge directly while a missionary in India for thirty-one years. For most of the history of missions in India, the gospel had essentially asked that people accept Christ and become British, American, Danish, etc. Unknown to many missionaries in that era, they carried with them a gospel of salvation that included the unbiblical requirement that converts change their ethnic, community, or family allegiance. This led to converts coming slowly to Christ, since most people saw Christianity as a Western religion that required them to abandon their own social networks.

It is a similar issue that confronted the disciples in Acts 15. Then, the question was, can a Gentile become a Christian without having to become a Jew? As the church spread among the Gentiles (Acts 11:20), the "word of the Lord continued to grow and to be multiplied" (Acts 12:24). Paul and Barnabas were sent forth on their first missionary journey and ended up turning primarily to the Gentiles (see Acts 13:46). After they returned to Antioch, they reported that "all things that God had done with them and how He had opened a door of faith to the Gentiles" (Acts 14:27). Almost immediately, some men began to preach and teach that the Gentiles had to abandon their own culture (read homogeneous unit) and become Jews (a different homogeneous unit). The question raised so much discussion that it was decided to go to Jerusalem to discuss the issue with the apostles and elders there. After arriving and entering into a very hot debate, it was finally decided, "We do not trouble those who are turning to God from among the Gentiles" (Acts 15:19). In other words it was determined that Gentiles could remain Gentiles (read "remain in their own homogeneous unit") and did not need to become Jews in order to be saved.

The Homogeneous Unit Principle states that, when it comes to evangelism, people desire to become Christian without leaving their homogeneous unit—their family, community, or ethnicity. The same issue has been a problem among Native American tribes in the United States. Few groups have had the gospel preached to them as diligently over so long a time as Native Americans. Yet only a small percentage of Native Americans are Christian believers. Why is this so? At least part of the answer, and maybe the main one, is that early Christian missionaries communicated that Native Americans had to accept Christ and become European whites (read Dutch, English, French, etc.). Since most Native Americans equated becoming Christian with becoming European, few accepted Christ. As McGavran later wrote, "It may be taken as axiomatic that whenever becoming a Christian is considered a racial rather than a religious decision, there the growth of the church will be exceedingly slow."[11] So today, we might ask whether a Nigerian can become a Christian and still be Nigerian. Or can a Korean become a Christian and still be Korean? Can an Egyptian become a Christian and still remain an Egyptian? McGavran put it this way, "As the Church faces the evangelization of the world, perhaps its main problem is how to present Christ so unbelievers can truly follow him without traitorously leaving their kindred."[12]

IS THE HOMOGENEOUS UNIT PRINCIPLE BIBLICAL?

We now understand that individuals must be viewed as individuals in social context, not as separate entities. The universal development of what is called social context or social structure began with the individual person of Adam (Gen. 1:27–28). But he (and his family afterward) could not exist alone (see Gen. 2:18). His essential aloneness caused Adam, and later other family members, to come together as couples and eventually form families. Families became extended families, or clans, eventually forming communities and societies. Social structure involves a community of communities, each with its right of existence.

As noted in an earlier chapter, the division of humankind into separate families, clans, and communities was part of the initial plan of God. God's command to Noah and his sons was, "Be fruitful and multiply, and *fill the earth*" (Gen. 9:1, emphasis added). But while they were in the process of moving into all parts of the world, some decided to disobey God and said, "Come, let us build for ourselves a city, and a tower whose top *will reach* into heaven, and let us make for ourselves a name, *otherwise we will be scattered abroad over the face of the whole earth*" (Gen. 11:4, emphasis added). Note that the people rebelled against God's clear command to fill the earth. God's judgment in confounding their language and scattering them over the face of the earth expedited what would have happened anyway if the people had followed his initial command to fill the earth. God accomplished in a moment what would have taken centuries. He punished them because they refused to be diverse! The fact is that God desired to see the nations (families, clans, communities) formed as one example of his own creativity. In some way, the manifold peoples of the world illustrate the multifaceted image of God. Thus, "He made from one *man* every nation of mankind to live on all the face of the earth, having determined *their* appointed times and the boundaries of their habitation" (Acts 17:26).

While God chose to create a diverse people, he also declared his love for them. But even his love toward all people was expressed through a single homogeneous unit—the family of Abram. To Abram God declared, "In you all the families of the earth will be blessed" (Gen. 12:3). Social structure (homogeneity) is a creation construct of God, and he works through it to reach the nations of the world.

God works within the social structure of mankind. For example, when Christ selected his twelve disciples, he could have appointed a diverse group of men. The area of Jerusalem certainly included a great diversity of people and included the following diverse people just among the Jews (there was additional diversity among the local Gentiles):

Cultural Distinctions	*Regional Identity: Hellenists*
Hebrews	Parthians
Hellenists	Medes
	Elamites
Religious Identity	Mesopotamians
Affiliation	Cappadocians
Pharisees	Asians
Sadducees	Phrygians
Essenes	Pamphylians
Hierarchy	Egyptians
Priests	Libyans
Levites	Romans
Laity	Cretans
	Arabs

But from this pool of potential diversity, Jesus narrowly chose eleven Aramaic-speaking Galileans, all of whom were religious laity. Only Judas Iscariot was not from Galilee but from Judea (Isscariot may mean "man from Judea"), and we know what happened to him. Later, when the disciples met to replace Judas Iscariot (see Acts 1:26), they picked Matthias, another Aramaic-speaking Galilean Jew. If Jesus had wished to destroy the idea of working within a homogeneous unit, this was a great opportunity to set a very clear example. But he chose his own kind—Galileans—to begin his work to reach the nations. Even the first ministry that Jesus sent the disciples on was limited to Galileans. "Do not go in *the* way of *the* Gentiles, and do not enter *any* city of the Samaritans; but rather go to the lost sheep of the house of Israel" (Matt. 10:5–6).

Though Christ worked in and through a narrow homogeneous group, he demonstrated love and concern for those outside such a limited circle. Yet, even when he reached those outside his own homogeneous unit, Christ won people in the context of winning the homogeneous group. The Samaritan woman at the well is an excellent example. Christ not only won her to faith but also the Samaritan group to which she belonged. After the Samaritan woman became convinced that Christ was the Messiah, she "left her water-pot, and went into the city and said to the men, 'Come, see a man who told me all the things that I *have* done; this is not the Christ, is it?'" (John 4:28–29). She returned to her own context, city, and homogeneous unit to testify of her faith. As the men were making their way out of the city to see for them-selves, Jesus called attention to them coming and said to his disciples, "Lift up your eyes and look on the fields, that they are white for harvest" (John 4:35). By this he made reference to the Samaritans coming out to see him. Later John writes, "From that city many of the Samaritans believed in Him because of the word of the woman" (John 4:39). Evangelism demands a context for converts since every person has a right to belong. Thus, a Samar-itan woman was brought to Christ amongst other members of her own homogeneous unit, many who also believed and who then likely established a community of faith where they could be nurtured together. This all hap-pened within the bounds of a clear homogeneous unit. It is important, how-ever, to note the existence of diversity within unity. While there was unity in their common ethnicity, there was also clear diversity—men and women, divorced and married. There is always homogeneity and heterogeneity.

The existence and acceptance of homogeneous units is also seen in the developing church in Acts 6. "While the disciples were increasing *in number*, a complaint arose on the part of the Hellenistic *Jews* against the *native* Hebrews, because their widows were being overlooked in the daily serving *of food*" (Acts 6:1). The growth of the church resulted in managerial diffi-culties that contained undertones of ethnic strife. One of the major challenges of numerical growth even today is how to care for the large number of peo-ple in a church. By this time, there may have been between fifteen thousand and twenty thousand believers in Jerusalem, which accounts for the prob-lems of food distribution. But the church was also more diverse, and Luke mentioned the cultural differences of Hellenists and native Hebrews. The problem was solved when the people selected their own leaders to manage the distribution of food. Surprisingly, while we might have expected them to choose a diverse group of leaders, they did just the opposite. The people selected and ordained seven indigenous leaders—Stephen, Philip, Prochorus, Nicanor, Timon, Parmenas, and Nicholas—all Hellenists. Once again, when the chance arose to set an example of diversity in leadership, the people were allowed to choose those of their own homogeneous unit, which they did without being criticized.

There is evidence of diversity in local churches, too. The churches in Antioch, Rome, and other places had some mixtures of slaves and free, Jews and Gentiles, and certainly males and females. Yet just as certainly, God creates the families, clans, and societies of the world, works within them to bring about his will, and allows his people to live within their own communities without impunity. Even the Great Commission as found in Matthew 28 and Luke 24 appears to require that churches be planted among all the homogeneous units of the world. We are commanded to "make disciples of all the nations" (Matt. 28:19). And it is written, "Repentance for forgiveness of sins would be proclaimed in His name to all the nations" (Luke 24:47). So how does one reach all the nations (literally all the ethnic families, clans, and communities of the world) unless churches are planted within all the homogeneous units of society?

If it is necessary to plant churches in all the units of society, how does this square with the main criticisms mentioned earlier? For instance, how can homogeneous units fit with Christ's High Priestly prayer for unity? In John 17 Christ prayed:

> I do not ask on behalf of these alone, but for those also who believe in Me through their word; that they may all be one; even as You, Father, *are* in Me and I in You, that they also may be in Us, so that the world may believe that You sent Me. The glory which You have given Me I have given to them, that they may all be one, just as We are one; I in them, and You in Me, that they may be perfected in unity, so that the world may know that You sent Me, and loved them, even as You have loved Me. (John 17:20–23)

The context of Christ's prayer is the fact that the disciples were being sent into the world and the reality that the world was going to hate the disciples because they were not of the world (John 17:13–18). Thus, Christ prayed for the Twelve, as well as all disciples who came after them, for protection. While unity in Christ ought to be visible in local churches, Christ's prayer for unity does not imply a mandate that all ethnic peoples in a given community must worship together in the same church. Merrill Tenney suggests, "A clear distinction should be drawn between four closely allied concepts: unanimity, uniformity, union, and unity. Unanimity means absolute concord of opinion within a given group of people. Uniformity is complete similarity of organization or ritual. Union implies political affiliation without necessarily including individual agreement. Unity requires oneness of inner heart and essential purpose, through the possession of a common interest or a common life."[13] The context of John 17 makes clear that the unity Christ prayed for is the oneness of inner heart and essential purpose, for he compared it to the unity between himself and the Father. The identity they have persists in oneness of nature, heart, and purpose, not physical togetherness. While worshiping together in one church service is one way of demonstrating unity, Christ's prayer goes beyond that to demonstrable unity of mind and heart among all believers in all places at all times. This can only be done on the inner heart level, and only partially on the local church level. Unity does not demand uniformity. The church of Christ can be both unified and diverse. People do not have to meet in the same groups to be unified.

Some criticize the homogeneity of churches something like the following. Since Colossians states that "there is no *distinction between* Greek and Jew, circumcised and uncircumcised, barbarian, Scythian, slave and freeman, but Christ is all, and in all" (Col. 3:11), we must all be in the same local church. Therefore only a heterogeneous church is biblical. Others quote the parallel passage in Galatians 3:28: "There is neither Jew nor Greek, there is neither slave nor free man, there is neither male nor female; for you are all one in Christ Jesus." Do these Scriptures mandate a heterogeneous (multi-ethnic) local church? We do not believe so.

It goes beyond the text to say that Paul's use of the contrasting words *Jew* and *Gentile*, *slave* and *free*, *male* and *female*, *circumcised* and *uncircumcised*, and *barbarian* and *Scythian* obliterates the principle of homogeneity. The context of both passages makes it clear that Paul was discussing the issues of religious privilege. In Colossians, Paul stated that all believers were to put aside sinful acts and attitudes such as, immorality, impurity, evil desire, greed, anger, wrath, abusive speech, and a few other things (Col. 3:5–9). The Colossians, and we too, put aside these evil practices (the old self) and put on the new self, which is being renewed according to the image of Christ. In this process of renewal, there is no special religious privilege. Paul said it made no difference whether one was Jew or Gentile, Greek or barbarian, slave or free; all were to be renewed to the point that Christ is all in all. The parallel passage in Galatians stresses the fact that there is no religious privilege when one comes to Christ. During the time of the Law, the Jews had special privilege. For example, Jewish men would sometimes thank God that "He did not make him a Gentile, a slave or a woman."[14] Paul then used the same three categories—neither Jew nor Greek, neither slave nor free, neither male nor female—to stress that we are all now children of God through faith in Christ Jesus. There is no longer any special privileged relationship with God. We feel that those critics who use these two passages to malign the Homogeneous Unit Principle misunderstand the intent of the texts.

Now, while these two passages do not obliterate homogeneous units as a created social construction by God, they do certainly mean a local church must not be racist, classist, or elitist. Speaking of the Colossian passage, Olsen declares, "The text makes clear that a local church which is racist, classist, and elitist is sinning against its very nature. Does this preclude homogeneous groups? It certainly does preclude *some* homogeneous churches . . . when homogeneity is predicated on pride, hatred, fear, selfish interests or some hierarchy of races concept."[15] However, we must add that an African-American church is not racist just because it is all black. A church whose membership is comprised primarily of union workers cannot be automatically classified as classist. Nor is an Asian church located near a university campus and composed of college professors and students to be labeled elitist. Just because some churches connect in a homogeneous context "does not lead to discrimination, racism or classism."[16] If we are forthright, we all must acknowledge that such sins are, sadly, possible in all kinds of churches—homogeneous and heterogeneous. Heterogeneous churches are not a magical cure for the sins of discrimination, racism, or classism. Unfortunately, church leaders who criticize homogeneous churches often appear to espouse a false idealism about the heterogeneous church. It is our belief, however, that when a biblical church—homogeneous or heterogeneous—emerges within the context imposed by geographical proximity, by ethnic considerations, by special calling or passion, and/or personal needs, it honors God.

A third question concerns the breaking down of the dividing wall of Ephesians 2:13–16, which states, "But now in Christ Jesus you who formerly were far off have been brought near by the blood of Christ. For He Himself is our peace, who made both *groups into* one and broke down the barrier of the dividing wall, by abolishing in His flesh the enmity, *which is* the Law of commandments *contained* in ordinances, so that in Himself He might make the two into one new man, *thus* establishing peace, and might reconcile them both in one body to God through the cross, by it having put to death the enmity." By this passage some writers assume that it is the responsibility of all local churches to witness to this reconciliation by practicing cultural and racial unity. However, there are major problems with such an interpretation.

First, the barrier is broken down by the abolishing of the law of commandments contained in ordinances, which implies that the alienation or wall was a theological one rather than one of prejudices or practices, although both were present. "The dividing wall of hostility was a function of the law, not racial and ethnic discrimination. The biblical theme of a Jew-Gentile reconciliation must be understood in the light of the covenant promises given to Abraham . . . not ethnic discrimination or racial prejudice."[17] The way is now open to all Gentiles to come to Christ. Paul declared that this is a great mystery (Eph. 3:3). The context, particularly Ephesians 3:6, tells us that the mystery was "that the Gentiles are fellow heirs and fellow members of the body, and fellow partakers of the promise in Christ Jesus through the gospel." Jews and Gentiles are now part of one body, the universal body of Christ. Will Jews and Gentiles worship together in the same local churches? Yes and no. But whether they do or do not worship in local churches together, they are still together part of the body. It is a fact that cannot be changed.

Second, the breaking down of the barrier is grammatically a once-and-for-all-time event. When Christ died on the cross, he broke down the barrier one time for all time and abolished the enmity one time for all time. It is now a historical fact that no barrier exists, no enmity exists. The passage also indicates that Christ once and for all time made the two one and reconciled them into one body. These are all things that have already been done in Christ. While the problems of racism, injustice, and inequality are real, this passage is not addressed to those problems. Of course, we must be about the work of justice, seeking to end racism, inequality, and a host of other sins in this world. Those are all part of our Christian duty. This passage, however, is speaking of what has already taken place through Christ.

Third, the reconciliation of which Paul spoke is the establishing of his universal church. The universal body of Christ could not have come into existence without the breaking down of the barrier between Jews and Gentiles. While Ephesians has words of praise and teaching for the saints at Ephesus, it goes beyond instructions to a local assembly and speaks to issues of the larger universal church. For example, Ephesians 1:22–23 speaks of Christ being placed as "head over all things to the church, which is His body, the fullness of Him who fills all in all." These two verses surely mean that Christ is head over the entire church—the universal church—rather than Christ is head of a single local church, say, in Ephesus. So, too, we believe Paul was talking about the universal church when he wrote, "You are fellow citizens with the saints, and are of God's household, having been built on the foundation of the apostles and prophets, Christ Jesus Himself being the corner *stone*" (Eph. 2:19–20). Were the Ephesians only fellow saints with each other, or with all the saints in God's household all over the world? Was it just the Ephesian church that was built on the foundation of the apostles and prophets, or was it the larger universal church? Is Christ just the cornerstone of the Ephesian church, or is he the cornerstone of the universal church? Obviously, Paul was talking about the larger, universal body of Christ, the church made up of all believers. When Paul opened the fourth chapter, he implored the Ephesians to walk worthy of their calling by being humble, patient, showing tolerance, and preserving the unity of the Spirit in the bonds of peace. This exhortation had immediate application to the Ephesians in their local assemblies, but also spoke to the universal church, as verses four through six demonstrate. Paul said, *"There is* one body" (Eph. 4:4). Is this one body not the larger universal church? Then Paul stated that Christ "gave some *as* apostles, and some *as* prophets, and some *as* evangelists, and some *as* pastors and teachers, for the equipping of the saints for the work of service, to the building up of the body of Christ" (Eph. 4:11–12). Again, these are gifts to the universal body of Christ to build up the universal church. Not spiritual gifts, but gifts of men who are for sure to engage their work in local churches, but in the context of the chapter, they are viewed as being given to the larger church.

Another criticism declares that local churches should mirror the eschatological church as described in Revelation: "After these things I looked, and behold, a great multitude which no one could count, from every nation and *all* tribes and peoples and tongues, standing before the throne and before the Lamb, clothed in white robes, and palm branches *were* in their hands; and they cry out with a loud voice, saying, 'Salvation to our God who sits on the throne, and to the Lamb'" (Rev. 7:9–10). It is important to see the verses in their context and that the passage is descriptive rather than prescriptive. John was simply telling what he saw, and in no sense did he tell the reader to do anything. His description was of the victorious martyrs who come out of the great tribulation (see Rev. 7:13–17). The passage points out two things. First, a great number of people will be saved during the tribulation. Second, they will represent people from all over the world— every nation, tribe, peoples, and tongues. Thus, the purpose of the passage is not to prescribe the necessity of multi-ethnic churches nor multicultural worship. To interpret the passage as teaching that churches today must be multi-ethnic takes the verses further than the context allows. However, a close reading reveals that the homogeneous units are still in place even in heaven. The fourfold description of nations, tribes, peoples, and tongues demonstrates that ethnic identities are still recognizable even in heaven. While the tribulation martyrs are gathered in praise to God for salvation, the fact that God has not done away with their ethnic identity argues for recognition of homogeneous units on earth.

The Great Commission demands that we go to all the nations (*ethne*), which means we are to establish local churches in every nation, tribe, clan, or culture in the world as a witness to the gospel of salvation in Christ Jesus alone. While we are in favor of establishing multi-ethnic churches where possible, this happens most often in urban centers of the world where the culture compresses the numerous homogeneous groupings closely together, thereby lowering people consciousness to a level where heterogeneous groups may be formed. In addition we are aware of no commission that requires us to break up cultures, social structures, tribes, or family units. In contrast, Scripture models acceptance and evangelistic labor that works in and through homogeneous units rather than against them.

True culture can only be born and sustained in a homogeneous environment. Therefore, even churches that are reportedly multi-ethnic, multiracial, or multicultural will, in time, become homogeneous. If they do not do so, they will not survive more than a generation. Churches may be formed for a variety of extrinsic and intrinsic reasons, which only have meaning when shared in a group context. Since heterogeneity is inherently unstable in regard to group formation, over time a heterogeneous group gradually becomes more and more homogeneous. Thus, there is really no such thing as a multicultural church, for to survive means a new homogeneous culture must be formed around which people can commonly agree.

What concerns us as missiologists is not the desire for multi-ethnic churches. In fact we rejoice in seeing multi-ethnic churches planted and established. But to categorically state that all churches must be multi-ethnic or multiracial or they are not biblical goes too far. By making such a statement, are not some passionate people saying that nearly all churches, past and present, are not biblical? We cannot go that far.

Instead it appears that the homogeneous church model is more biblical than heterogeneous churches. If heterogeneity is the biblical model, why do we not see more churches that are heterogeneous? After nearly two thousand years of Christian history, has the church failed so greatly in missing the mark of what Christ wants in his church; or is it that heterogeneity is to be the norm in the universal church, which is extremely heterogeneous, while homogeneity is to be the norm in the local church? Is this not the more biblical model?

We tend to agree with Walther Olsen, who writes, "Our Heavenly Father *leads his sheep to folds prepared to nurture them.* For those who bear his Son's Name, God desires a church life which will be for their redemptive good in the face of life's troubling issues and the perplexities of the human condition. A milieu that will sustain their personhood and give them a self-identity. Homogeneous churches are born in this matrix."[18]

PUTTING INSIGHTS TO WORK

1. What evidence do you see of homogeneous units in your church? How do your people tend to gather in classes, groups, or meetings? Whom do your people tend to fellowship with outside of church?

2. Do you believe the Homogeneous Unit Principle is biblical or not? What is your support for your belief?

3. In what ways is your church heterogeneous? In what ways is it homogeneous? Assuming the primary glue that holds people together in your church is their love for Christ, what is the secondary glue, or homogeneity, that binds them together?

8

IMMIGRANT CHURCHES

Give me your tired, your poor, your huddled masses yearning to breathe free, the wretched refuse of your teeming shore. I lift my lamp beside the golden door.
—Emma Lazarus

It does not take much effort these days to recognize that your neighborhood has changed from how it was a few decades ago. In the 1960s and 1970s when someone referred to a minority group in town, they usually were referring to the African-American population, and the primary questions revolved around racial tensions, the issues of segregation, and the unequal opportunities it created. Today, most Americans know they are as likely to find in their neighborhoods Asian immigrants, Middle Eastern people, Latinos, or African immigrants who each speak a different language. While racial tensions still exist, most of the new immigrant groups have little memory of civil rights violations and the sense of powerlessness they created.

Today, according to statistics released by the Population Division of the United Nations, there are approximately two hundred million international migrants in the world.[1] That figure represents a population the size of the nation of Brazil that is currently on the move from where they once lived, to a new country of residence. The number of international migrants has doubled since 1980, and if it continues to increase at the rate it has in the last five years, by the year 2050 the number of international migrants will be as high as 405 million.[2]

A disproportionate number of these international migrants are women, often traveling independently and as heads of households. This pattern is quite different than what it was a few years ago when men more typically than women traveled across international boundaries to seek employment so they could send financial resources back to their families. Another new fact is that the ethnic and cultural diversity of these migrants is higher than it has ever been in history, with the flow accelerating from the Southern Hemisphere to the Northern Hemisphere and from rural areas to the city.

The United States remains the leading destination for immigrants in the world, receiving a total of thirty-eight million international migrants (20 percent of the worldwide total) in 2005. Russia is the second destination with twelve million and Germany third with ten million.[3] From 1995 to 2000 a full 75 percent of the population growth in the US came from immigration.[4] The disproportionate migration to Western nations is seen in the fact that one out of three international migrants live in Western Europe and one out of four live in North America.[5]

For many immigrants, the first place of residence is in a city, especially gateway cities such as Miami, Los Angeles, New York, Chicago, and San Francisco. These cities represent ports of entry for newcomers. Miami represents the city with the most foreign born of any city in North America with 59 percent, followed by Toronto at 50 percent,[6] and New York at 36 percent.[7] New York City is home to an estimated 170 nationalities speaking approximately eight hundred languages[8] while in Los Angeles, 224 different languages are spoken by 140 nationalities.[9]

After a period of adjustment, many new immigrants decide to make the city their permanent home and raise their families there. Some may move to a secondary, less expensive destination where others from their nation or culture have congregated. Surprisingly, a few immigrants choose to reside in secondary hubs, smaller cities that are not usually considered hotbeds of immigrants. For example, today, large concentrations of Hmong people from Laos are found in Fresno, California; Macedonians live in Garfield, New Jersey; and Dearborn, Michigan, houses large Muslim populations.

From the perspective of mission strategy, these population trends are remarkable. In urban contexts, especially, these population centers offer a level of efficiency and opportunity for evangelism not found anywhere else. Central locations allow for multiple nationalities to be reached with the gospel. Because many of these people are recent transplants and are open to establishing new connections and interests, many of them are receptive to considering new ideas. In fact some returning missionaries actually find more receptivity in ministering to international migrants in the US than when they are ministering to the same people in their native lands! For example, one colleague with whom Alan worked found more opportunities to minister among West African immigrants in New York City than he did when he was serving in West Africa with the Southern Baptists.[10]

In order to respond to this opportunity, churches, mission agencies, and nongovernment organizations (NGOs) need to rethink their approaches in ministering in the multi-ethnic context of our cities. They also need to study how to establish both inclusive mono-ethnic churches as well as multi-ethnic churches with the realization that each type of church is best designed to reach particular people. In most situations, mono-ethnic churches are best for reaching first generation immigrants because they offer the fewest number of cultural hurdles to overcome while the immigrants adjust to a new life in the United States. Multi-ethnic churches, on the other hand, provide a more attractive environment for second generation, bicultural young people who are coming to appreciate the new level of diversity, as well as feeling pressures to conform to the dominant culture in school, sports, and the marketplace.

CREATIVE TENSIONS

Of particular relevance to the discussion of immigrant churches are the issues of enculturation, acculturation, assimilation, and multiculturalism. Enculturation is the process by which we learn what is acceptable and normal for our culture. The process begins at birth and continues throughout one's life. Enculturation is how we are socialized by our parents and peers to become acceptable members of society. It is the ways we learn our first culture (and for most of us there is only one first culture), that of our parents. Second-generation immigrants may have two first cultures to learn, that of their parents and that of the new host culture they encounter at school.

Acculturation is the process through which we learn a second culture, and it occurs as two cultures interact with each other. Usually minority groups are expected to acculturate to the values and cultural norms of the dominant group. But the reality is that, as two cultures come into contact with each other, both groups are altered and pick up the flavor of the other. This process of interacting with other cultures can either enhance the richness of one's own culture or dilute it depending on one's perspective. Immigrants look at acculturation differently depending on their age at the point of immigration, their life cycle, or other issues as we will see shortly. The reality is that immigrants must deal with both issues simultaneously. The big issue with most immigrants is how to maintain the identity of family, culture, and religion, while at the same time learning and adapting to the culture of the new land.

Similar tensions can be found in assimilation and multiculturalism. Assimilation assumes or actively encourages minorities to adopt the values of the dominant culture and ethnicity. Consider one example from the early years of America. In the history of the United States, assimilation policies sanctioned the forcible removal of Native American children from their parents and their registration into boarding schools where learning to speak, read, and write English, as well as adopting American values would, as believed in those times, civilize them. These methods were perceived to be necessary in order to help disadvantaged people become self-supporting and functioning members of society.

Multiculturalism, on the other hand, seeks to recognize, appreciate, and advocate for multiple cultures operating in a common context so that each group has equal access to resources and is fairly represented in governance (often requiring some measure of affirmative action). In contrast to assimilation strategies, which seek to combine ethnicities, multiculturalism seeks to celebrate or even emphasize differences. In multiculturalism, no one group is held as superior to the others or given privileged status. It is often contrasted to assimilationist policies that seek to conform minority groups to those values held by majority groups.

While these two models, assimilation (the melting-pot approach) or multiculturalism (the salad-bowl approach), propagate different visions, multiculturalism seems superior on the surface. And, in fact, most multi-ethnic church advocates agree.

However, problems exist with either approach. On the one hand, multiculturalism suggests that, with competing values and worldviews, no one group has the right to define the rules or dictate theology, ecclesiology, or any other culturally defined norm. This assumption has led to moral relativism and threatens to fracture the social fabric of society. Opponents of multiculturalism argue that, unless there is a cohesive social identity, society as we know it will fly apart. The same is true in a church or a neighborhood. Infinite diversity without some commonly held value or set of assumptions makes communication and decision-making impossible. Even in a democratic process, the majority group, by the sheer power of its collective will, dictates the rules for the minorities. But who says that the democratic process should be the way decisions are made? Honoring another ethnic tradition may demand that consensus or elder authority is the basis on which decisions are made.

Assimilation models introduce their own set of problems. Assimilation strategies assume (or demand) that newcomers or minorities adopt the practices and values of those who are in power due to numbers, wealth, or position. Students of history know that those with power tend to abuse it, even when they think they are serving others. The same can happen in multi-ethnic churches where, in spite of honorable intentions, they operate by a set of rules—whether it is the way worship services are conducted or the way decisions are made— that favor those who are already in positions of power or were there first.

In the end, we are not left with clear solutions to these dilemmas, but shades of grey. How much does an immigrant population enculturate rather than acculturate? How does a multi-ethnic church balance the need to assimilate newcomers into a common theology and practice, versus recognizing and valuing all that each contributing ethnic group has to offer, with the goal of moving to a higher expression of God's will for his people? The answers to these questions evade quick solutions, even for those who are intentional about crossing cultural boundaries and welcoming others. Perhaps one strength of a multi-ethnic church is that it teaches us to tolerate such ambiguities and learn to bask in the creative tension these questions produce. While we may not be able to solve all of these problems, by struggling with the issues, we are now confused at a higher level and about more important things than we were before. And that is progress!

IMMIGRANT PARTICIPATION IN MULTI-ETHNIC CHURCHES

A common language has emerged for talking about immigrants at different stages of assimilation. The term *1.0 immigrants* refers to people who were born in a different country, may only speak their native tongue (or have limited English skills), and refer back to their native culture for their values. When we speak of *2.0 immigrants,* we refer to those who were born in the new host country and are more likely to speak the dominant language, and may have limited ability to speak in the native tongue of their parents. They desire to follow the cultural patterns dominant in the new host country and often seek to distance themselves from the old traditional values of their parents. The term *1.5 immigrants* refers to those born in their parents' native country but who moved to a new country when they were still children. Depending on how old they were when they moved, they may have varying degrees of allegiance to or language aptitude for either the native country or the new host culture. The 1.5s often have the most difficult time knowing which culture they belong to and what rule set to follow. But they also represent the best bridge people to help the 1.0s and the 2.0s understand each other.

In establishing churches that serve the needs of each of these groups, it is clear that one size does not fit all. The 1.0 immigrants fear the loss of important social and cultural values, religious beliefs, and identity. Forcing them to assimilate into a foreign culture (even if they live in this foreign land) often builds a stiff resistance that may result in a withdrawal from the mainstream of society and their moving into a ghetto or neighborhood where the food, dress styles, places of worship, and social institutions are all familiar. Establishing mono-ethnic churches, worship services, or small groups is often the easiest way to reach them and meet their needs. Mono-ethnic church plants specifically designed to reach these populations are often the best way to engage them with the gospel of Jesus Christ. When a multi-ethnic model of the church is used, homogeneous groups for 1.0 immigrants are still created so they can worship in their own language and culture without having to give up their identity in order to find Christ. This mono-ethnic approach existing inside a multi-ethnic church respects the 1.0 individuals as unique expressions of God's creation and seriously contextualizes the gospel. The challenge is to help 1.0 individuals move toward inclusive mono-ethnicity with the result that they become more accepting and appreciative of other ethnicities and eventually work to overcome the cultural barriers that divide the generations and the nations.

The 2.0 immigrants usually follow one of four patterns in church attendance. First, they remain in a mono-ethnic (1.0) church but with stress because the church does not help them address the problems they face in the larger society. In their effort to please their parents, they remain at odds with the rest of society, or in an opposite reaction, they leave the church altogether.

The second pattern is they assimilate into a dominant culture church (for example, a Caucasian service) and seek to minimize their identity as 2.0 immigrants. In this case they often live life as two different people, with one face to the dominant culture and one face to their parents. In this case, they make the church they are attending multi-ethnic (by some measures), though that church's worship service, evangelism, and discipleship structures may be driven by the dominant culture. Their very presence creates a kind of multi-ethnicity, though at times this is beyond the knowledge or intention of the church that receives them.

A third pattern results when the 2.0s join a church composed largely of other 2.0 immigrants (mono-ethnic) where they do not need to explain themselves either to their parents or the larger, more dominant culture. They are at home. Although their church experience may represent some level of fusion between their native culture and their level of adaptation to the new host culture.

The fourth pattern is that they join a multi-ethnic church where the goal of creating a heterogeneous congregation is given serious attention in the worship service, discipleship ministries, and leadership structures and styles. These churches, though quite intentional about blending the cultures at some levels, often use a combination of multi-ethnic gatherings (worship services) and mono-ethnic groupings (language-specific services or homogeneous small groups).

Very often 1.5 immigrants remain in a 1.0 church but serve as a bridge builder to the 2.0 immigrants by either functioning on the English service leadership team or as a youth pastor (leader) to 2.0 immigrants. In the building of a multi-ethnic church, 1.5 immigrants are a valuable asset because they have already learned how to negotiate between two competing worldview systems. It is on these individuals that new, collaborative ministries are best constructed to help the generations and ethnicities move toward mutual acceptance and support.

The immigration stages (1.0, 1.5, and 2.0) also help us understand how an immigrant's life stage relates to a multi-ethnic church model. First-generation immigrants (1.0) typically seek social spaces that offer some degree of familiarity because they are easily overwhelmed with the unfamiliar everywhere else. For many, a church designed to minister to their cultural group becomes a place of safety and acceptance. A homogeneous (mono-ethnic) church or fellowship group offers the best support for them during their early years in a new country. Their ability to participate in more multi-ethnic gatherings increases as they develop confidence in their own ability to navigate the social spaces of the new host culture. But this usually takes place after they raise their children to a point of independence. As their children start to pull away from the traditional cultures of the parents, the parents are often more willing to participate in a multi-ethnic context. In fact, multi-ethnic churches are particularly good at providing both mono-ethnic clusters while creating a larger multi-ethnic context. This serves the needs of the immigrant family because it allows the parents to attend a mono-ethnic worship service while their children participate in a multi-ethnic youth group or college group. In this fashion, all family members have a space that fits their needs but all attend the same church.

Often 1.5 or 2.0 immigrants are more receptive to being involved in a multi-ethnic or foreign-culture-dominated church beginning with their teen years and continuing until they start having children. For many this period lasts through college, early career entry, and the first years of marriage. During this period of time they are more flexible, more culturally curious, and more willing to make the investment to adapt to or accept the values of other cultural groups. But for many, things change when they start having children. At that point, many immigrants feel a need to anchor their children in more traditional cultural values (that of their parents) in order to give their children a more solid cultural identity.[11] While in their earlier years of increasing personal independence, they are willing to participate in a multi-ethnic church. In their child-rearing years, they become less likely to seek cultural values or identities outside their own ethnic group. In some cases, after the children are grown and move on, the 1.5 or 2.0 immigrants may again be more willing to participate in heterogeneous (multi-ethnic) churches. Thus, not only is the age of the immigrant important (regarding when he or she first arrived in the new country), but so is the life stage. When they are less responsible for child rearing, their potential for involvement in a multi-ethnic church increases. The following figure seeks to capture these patterns in a graphical format.

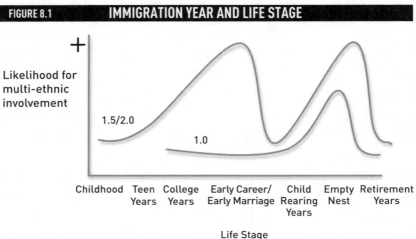

FIGURE 8.1   IMMIGRATION YEAR AND LIFE STAGE

Likelihood for multi-ethnic involvement

1.5/2.0

1.0

Childhood Teen Years College Years Early Career/ Early Marriage Child Rearing Years Empty Nest Retirement Years

Life Stage

LIKELIHOOD OF IMMIGRANT INVOLVEMENT IN MULTI-ETHNIC CHURCHES

Like receptivity to the gospel waxes and wanes for people and nations, so does one's personal receptivity to participation in multi-ethnic gatherings (church services, small groups, congregations). As immigrants become more adjusted and more at home with life in cultural contexts other than their own, they become better able to appreciate and participate with other cultures.

Other factors also affect an immigrant's likelihood to participate in a multi-ethnic church. Social pressure from one's ethnic group where faith and culture are tightly intertwined can decrease the willingness to be involved with other cultures. For example, many Indonesians believe that to be Indonesian is to be Muslim, and the same holds true for a variety of Protestant believers who, because of ethnocentrism, believe that their way of practicing the Christian faith is the only right way. Likewise, an immigrant's prior context may influence his or her eagerness to participate in a multi-ethnic church. Those from a cosmopolitan, urban environment are predictably more open to multi-ethnic church environments than those who come from tribal or rural areas. In the same way, an immigrant's educational background, economic status, or occupation can influence how he or she engages with multi-ethnic churches.

The goal of the pastoral staff in both mono-ethnic and multi-ethnic churches should be to recognize where different people are in their journey to becoming more culturally inclusive, and to serve them in a way that is appropriate to what God is doing in their hearts and lives. In each case, the staff needs to help people take the next step toward being inclusive and accepting of other cultures. Should the next step for an individual be at a crawl, a walk, or a run in the journey of becoming more accepting and empowering of other cultures? Answering that question will take spiritual discernment, a good understanding of how people make the adjustments toward being more multicultural, and a clear picture of what increasing levels of healthy multiculturalism looks like.

MEASUREMENTS OF ASSIMILATION

Assimilation, at some level, is virtually inevitable the longer an immigrant remains in a new land, even when there is little pressure to do so. In fact, rather than minorities simply assimilating the values of the majority culture, the process of converging into a new common identity happens for all ethnicities that are engaged in social exchange. Acculturation of each group toward the values of the others is happening all the time in multicultural contexts. Rap music, with its roots in African oral culture, has gone mainstream and has defined, in part, the contemporary urban psyche. Food trucks selling fusion food (for example, kimchi burritos) are now popular in Los Angeles.

What happens in society also happens in the multi-ethnic church. Dirke Johnson, referencing the work of sociologist James Lull,[12] states,

When two or more cultures come together, a new and different culture will form—which may have elements of the represented cultures but is really unique in and of itself. For example, a group that has a Black, White, and Latino cultural mix may have elements of each culture in the group. However, to make room for all three expressions, the group's culture will differ from a group that had one primary cultural expression. A multicultural group cannot experience the same cultural expression of worship that a monocultural group experiences. The multicultural group experiences a hybrid version and creates its own culture. To demand that all cultural expressions merge together will only, over time, diminish and eliminate those cultural expressions.[13]

For the immigrant, assimilation to the host or dominant culture(s) happens gradually over a period of several generations. The people in the first generation most often speak limited English and speak the mother tongue at home and with their people. Those in the second generation tend to be bilingual, shifting their language depending on whom they are talking to. The third generation speaks mostly English and very little of the mother tongue. So for most immigrant groups, full assimilation occurs by the third generation, though a number of factors are at play that may alter the speed of this process for some groups.

Standard measures of immigration assimilation, developed and used by sociologists, document the rate and amount of absorption into a dominant society: socioeconomic status, spatial concentration, language assimilation, and intermarriage.[14] By looking at these sets of factors, social scientists are able to assess how much immigrant groups identify with a dominant culture.

Socioeconomic status examines such factors as educational achievement, trade specialization, and earning equivalences. Census data collected and examined over a period of several years concludes that it takes immigrants approximately twenty years of residence in the United States to catch up with the majority population.[15] Certain immigrant groups outperformed native whites (for example, the Chinese population in terms of high school graduation rates) and some lagged behind (for example, third-generation Mexican immigrants).

Studies focusing on spatial concentration point out that most new immigrants first settle in the large gateway cities mentioned earlier and only over time begin to distribute out over a larger region. As immigrant groups become more successful and acclimate to their new surroundings, their population densities begin to drop as they migrate to suburban areas and secondary cities. Research also shows that blacks experience the highest levels of segregation from whites, while Latino and Asian populations are only moderately segregated.[16]

In terms of linguistic patterns, studies show that language ability rapidly improves the longer the immigrant is in the United States. By the third generation, two-thirds to three-fourths of immigrant populations no longer speak any of the language of their parents.[17] Language patterns of the succeeding generations changed much faster than worldview assumptions.

Finally, the rates of intermarriage between the races serve for many as the ultimate test of assimilation. In effect, the highest levels of acceptance and tolerance of multi-ethnic contexts occur when people are willing to have their children marry someone from another ethnic group. Studies show much higher intermarriage rates between whites and Asians and whites and Latinos than would be true between blacks and whites. As a general pattern, however, there is a higher likelihood that someone will marry another person from the same broad group (Chinese with Koreans or Puerto Ricans with Mexicans) than to marry outside the broad ethnic group altogether.[18]

In recent years another pattern has emerged among immigrant groups that in some ways mimics the role religion has traditionally played. *Side-stream ethnicity* or *symbolic ethnicity*[19] is the term given to the way ethnic identity is used to position oneself as a mainstream American, especially among second-generation immigrants. People's ethnicity and cultural peculiarities give them an autonomous identity to express their individualism. Such an identity allows them to take their seat at the multicultural table without either having to give up their ethnic identity or feel ostracized from the mainstream of society. Side-stream ethnicity serves to create an accepted social space that does not have to constantly explain itself either to the minority or majority population.

Taken collectively, this data shows that assimilation takes time and is manifested in a variety of ways. Multi-ethnic churches are often preferred by those immigrants further along in the assimilation process who wish to break free from the constraints of the traditional, mono-ethnic immigrant churches of their parents. However, rather than just serving the needs of the 1.5 and 2.0 immigrants, they can also provide, through mono-ethnic sub-groupings (worship services, small groups, etc.), a place for the 1.0s as well. Rather than shaping the dialogue to pit mono-ethnic churches against multi-ethnic churches, a wiser strategy is to consider how each church type serves the needs of some audience particularly well. By recognizing this fact and working together cooperatively, churches can maximize their individual strengths as well as the unique contributions that others bring. This cooperation can be done inside a single multi-ethnic church that strategically utilizes homogeneous and heterogeneous units. Or it can be done on a regional level as mono-ethnic churches work closely with other mono-ethnic or multi-ethnic churches to serve the needs of the different generations of immigrant populations. Whether on the micro or macro level, the scriptural mandate is to be inclusive to all ethnicities that come through our doors and to be proactive to cross ethnic, linguistic, and social barriers to go to those who do not. This dual mode of engagement with the nations captures both the centripetal nature of evangelism as practiced in the Old Testament and the centrifugal nature of evangelism from the New Testament.

PUTTING INSIGHTS TO WORK

1. Do you know any persons who are immigrants to the United States? If so, in what ways have you observed creative tensions, like those mentioned in this chapter, in their lives?

2. Do the immigrant peoples in your community primarily represent the 1.0, 1.5, or 2.0 immigrants? What level of assimilation do you observe among ethnic peoples in your church's ministry area? What does this mean for your church's evangelism strategy?

3. Based on the immigration patterns described in this chapter, what approach to being a multi-ethnic church seems the best for your church? Why is this so?

URBAN CHURCHES

Urban churches have been on the leading edge of the multi-ethnic waves throughout history. A key reason for this fact is that the neighborhoods in which urban churches are located are already highly diverse. In most cases, if the church is attempting to represent the composition of the neighborhood, it must be multi-ethnic to some degree.

The diversity of the city is caused by intersecting factors that together make urban ministry a highly strategic place to reach the nations for Christ. One factor is the sheer population growth that cities are experiencing. Beginning in 2008, for the first time in history, more of the world's people lived in cities than not. By the year 2050, it is estimated that the global urban population will increase by 3.1 billion people to reach a total of 6.5 billion or 70 percent of all the people on earth.[1] In the United States by that same year, it is estimated that 90 percent of all Americans will live in cities. If you want to do ministry where the people are, the city will be the place to be.

Second, the nations of the world are moving to the city. The Population Division of the United Nations estimates that worldwide there are two hundred million international migrants on the move today.[2] That figure is approximately the size of the nation of Brazil and it is twice the number of international migrants in 1980. By 2050, this number could double to 405 million.[3] More than half of that population is made up of women as heads of households, and the general direction of flow is from the Southern to the Northern Hemisphere and from the rural areas to the urban context. The United States is the number one immigration destination receiving about 20 percent of the worldwide total (thirty-eight million).[4] The cities in North America that have the greatest percentages of foreign born are Miami with 59 percent, Toronto with 50 percent,[5] and New York with 36 percent.[6] New York plays host to approximately 170 nationalities speaking eight hundred languages[7] while Los Angeles is home to 140 nationalities, speaking 224 different languages.[8] Clearly, cities are the crossroads of the world. Relatively small geographic space combined with high population density and high diversity makes the city a strategic place to do ministry in a multi-ethnic way.

Functioning as immigration ports of entry, cities are often the first place immigrants choose to reside. In the city, they find a number of appealing features. First among these is the reality that in the city they find others from their same culture. In the urban ethnic neighborhoods, they will find people who speak their language, eat their food, remember the cultural and national traditions of the homeland, and perhaps offer them employment. In time, these new migrants may move on to a secondary destination in the United States where they will establish more permanent roots. However, many will stay in the city where they first landed and make that their home. The city, then, becomes not a melting pot as was once thought, but a stew pot of cultures, each maintaining its cultural uniqueness while flavoring the others.

Successive waves of immigration into a city mean that many neighborhoods undergo ethnic shifts. Harlem, in New York City, was largely composed of lower-class Jewish and Italian immigrants in the 1800s. Increasingly, it became identified with African-Americans who started moving to the area en masse in 1904. Today that same neighborhood is the destination of Hispanics and more affluent whites. Koreatown in Los Angeles was once the home of movie stars and the well-to-do before becoming the center of Korean immigration in the 1970s. Now Latinos make up more than half of the population.

PATTERNS OF RESPONSE

As people of different cultures and ethnicities interact in the city, different response patterns are observed. For some immigrants, their place of worship becomes the center of their community and cultural identity. It is here that they seek and find the familiar in a strange and alien land. The place of worship—be it a temple, mosque, synagogue, or church—is a safe haven to meet with people like oneself, remember the cultural holidays, eat the comfort foods from home, speak the mother tongue, and have sons and daughters meet people from their own ethnic background. These houses of worship are typically mono-ethnic, not out of hatred of others, but because those who attend are desperate to preserve their roots in a place where everything has changed. Often their faith identity becomes synonymous with their ethnic identity. For example, to be Indonesian is to be Muslim, and to be Romanian is to be Eastern Orthodox. While others may criticize their assemblies as being too ethnically defined, the fact of the matter is that there is only so much diversity one can tolerate. Accommodation and adjustment to the host culture takes months, years, or generations before immigrants make the new context their home.

A second typical response pattern to cross-cultural contact in the city is more easily observed in the faith patterns of second-generation immigrants. As school-aged children of immigrant families enter the public school system, they experience strong pressures to conform to the social norms of the dominant culture. Over time they tend to pull back from the traditional ways of their parents as a means of surviving in the new world. Distancing themselves more and more from the heavy cultural presence of their parents' place of worship, they are more likely to be "lost" from the faith, to become more secular in their orientation. Those young people who come from Christian families may seek affiliation with churches that are large enough to contain wider ethnic representation but are driven by values and worship styles of the dominant culture. A majority of the churches in the United States that have multi-ethnic attendance in worship are nevertheless mono-cultural in their worship style and ministry expressions.

A third response pattern to the cross-cultural soup of the city is to find places of worship that truly celebrate the diversity of the neighborhood. Churches that utilize worship, discipleship, evangelism, and leadership patterns typical of multiple cultures often do so without any specific intentionality. They are simply reflecting the diversity of their people without critical examination of why they do what they do. At times it may simply reflect the various personalities or cultural backgrounds of their leadership. Alternatively, their cultural intelligence (their tolerance of and adaptability to varying cultural expressions) may be so high that they move easily from one cultural form to another without much thought. In many cases, however, churches that mix cultural styles in their worship services and ministry approaches do so intentionally to make people of multiple cultures feel at home and to celebrate the rich diversity of the human family.

A fourth response pattern that is more typical of urban ministry contexts rather than rural ones, is the recent phenomenon in which people attend multiple churches, each for a different reason. For example, they may attend one church periodically because of an excellent choir. They then attend a small group sponsored by a different church. In still another church, their kids attend a vibrant youth group. In one multi-ethnic church in Los Angeles, Alan talked with a man after a service who indicated that he attended four churches on a revolving basis. He was attending one particular church every second Sunday of the month. In urban contexts where the geographical distances are not great and churches are readily available, some create their own multi-ethnic diversity by being involved in multiple churches that each fulfill a unique need in the life of the attendee.

Population increases, combined with diversity brought by international migration and demographic shifts within long-established neighborhoods, create a rich ethnic blend that naturally finds its way into a church. Some churches become increasingly multi-ethnic by simply welcoming visitors from minority populations and then adjusting their worship styles and leadership staffing to match the ethnic blends of the congregation. Other congregations become quite intentional to reach out to ethnic groups that are locally close but culturally distant. They may see themselves as a church with a missional agenda to carry the gospel to every people, or as a reconciliation church that will model for the community what oneness in Christ looks like. In either case these churches move with deliberate intention to create a multi-ethnic church.

CATEGORY WIDTH

In developing and growing multi-ethnic churches, urban contexts have a special advantage. An illustration will help to make the point. Alan grew up in a small, racially divided town in North Carolina where the different races had been polarized against each other, making it difficult to mix the black and white populations together. But when he went to the New York City area for college, he encountered a large multiplicity of ethnic groups. In a city where a large percentage of the population was foreign-born and originated from many different countries, the black and white polarity he experienced in North Carolina was not as intense. In New York City, it seemed that one's ethnicity made less difference. The great diversity of the city had created a greater category width among its inhabitants.

The term *category width* describes how many events or items one puts under a single label. For example, how many colors fit under our label of "blue"? Most of us have been taught to think there are twelve basic colors: three primary colors of red, yellow, and blue; three secondary colors obtained by combining the primary colors: green, orange, and purple; and six tertiary colors made by combining primary and secondary colors.[9] So, how close to purple can you go before something is no longer blue but purple? How you answer that question might depend on your culture. One ethnic culture uses only four words for color: *black*, *white*, *dry*, and *wet*. In that color spectrum, where do you put the color blue? Pick up a paint chart from your local hardware store. How many names for blue can you find and when does a blue become a gray on the paint chart? Category width helps us determine how broad our definition of blue can be.

Category width . . . is distinct in that it specifically looks at how cultures socialize their members to tolerate things that don't neatly fall into one category or another. Category width exposes the reality that individuals, largely due to cultures in which they are socialized, differ consistently in the extent to which they use broad or narrow categories for labeling the world. Some people are consistently wide categorizers, while others are consistently narrow. The hypothesis is that the breadth one uses in categorizing things extends across all types of judgments. Going deep to see how we think about things that don't neatly conform to our experience and understanding is an essential part of the interpretive [cultural intelligence] process.[10]

It can also help us know how tolerant we are of others of a different ethnicity. People who use narrow categories emphasize the differences. They observe the behavior of people from a different culture and compare it to a subconscious set of criteria. If the item or behavior does not fit into their categories, they judge it to be an exception or quickly label it as right or wrong. Conversely, people who use broad categories focus on the ways items or behaviors are similar. They can more easily tolerate discrepancies or exceptions to a rule. They see exceptions to the usual rules as simply being different, not better or worse or abnormal.

FIGURE 9.1	CATEGORY WIDTH[11]

Narrow Categorizers

Right	Different	Wrong

Broad Categorizers

Right	Different	Wrong

In urban contexts where people are regularly exposed to tremendous individual variation, ranging from a Hmong immigrant family to "razorhead" skateboarders to young, middle-class female "fashionistas," the category width tends to be wider. This growing tolerance of people unlike us gives opportunity for new innovations and trends to develop. As a result, urban contexts are often the birthplace of new trends, fashions, and social norms. That the multi-ethnic church tends to thrive in the city should not be surprising. Like many other trends, as diversity continues to spread throughout the country into ever smaller cities and towns, the urban multi-ethnic church may foreshadow and model what other churches could expect to see in the future.

Earlier we said that cities are getting bigger as more and more people are moving into urban contexts. A corollary of size is density. As the number of people increases in a city, the more they compete for certain scarce resources. Entrepreneurs see the opportunity and build bigger and taller buildings, thus increasing the number of people per square mile.[12] Predictions now say that by the middle of this century (2050) the world's total urban population will be the size of the entire world's population in 2004.[13] This ever-increasing density creates opportunity.

When urban populations are compressed together, the social patterns of its inhabitants begin to change. Large numbers of people coming together in one place increase the likelihood that they will encounter a large number of people of diverse backgrounds and lifestyle preferences. This dissimilarity manifests itself in higher variations in race, culture, economic capability, and class types. Multi-ethnic churches respond to this diversity by reducing the relative influence of any one dominant cultural group. Churches whose attendance is composed of people from widely varying backgrounds suggest that they have a place for one more person who is different, even if there are few attendees from one's own cultural group. Multi-ethnic churches communicate a broad category width that makes newcomers feel more welcome, even if there is no worship service in their language. Because of their broad category width, multi-ethnic urban churches embrace the otherness that is a part of the city. As a result, they diminish the social distance that separates people by ethnicity or class. By being more tolerant of ethnic diversity, multi-ethnic churches suggest that their congregations are also more tolerant of other types of diversity such as economic, generational, or educational.

One example of this broader category width is the large, urban, ethnic church that consolidates multiple ethnicities that are a part of the same cultural family block into one congregation. For example, New Song Church in Irvine, California, is by most definitions an Asian church. Though their worship service is in English, it attracts a mix of second-, third-, and fourth-generation Chinese, Korean, Japanese, Vietnamese, and other Asians to form a congregation of more than seven hundred.[14] Interestingly enough, it does not attract many Caucasian (17 percent), or African-American and Latino attendees (3 percent combined).[15] This church illustrates that a broad category width is what attracted other kinds of people to its services, even when their ethnicities did not match. Even though their racial and ethnic identities diverged, enough commonalities existed to draw them together. For example, the average age of the members was twenty-eight, 15 percent were college age, and 65 percent were single.[16] However, category width is not infinitely wide because some ethnicities (those with Arabic, Spanish, or Russian roots) were not inclined to come to this church. So all churches, including multi-ethnic churches, have a certain bandwidth in which they effectively communicate. It would seem that churches like New Song are communicating in a bandwidth that attracts a pan-Asian crowd. But that same frequency does not work as well with ethnicities that are not Asian.

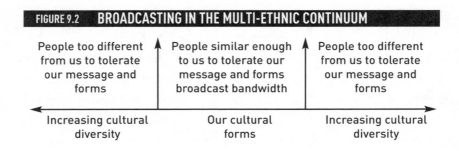

FIGURE 9.2   BROADCASTING IN THE MULTI-ETHNIC CONTINUUM

People too different from us to tolerate our message and forms	People similar enough to us to tolerate our message and forms broadcast bandwidth	People too different from us to tolerate our message and forms
Increasing cultural diversity	Our cultural forms	Increasing cultural diversity

Every church has developed an audience that is drawn to the message and forms of its ministries. A careful study of a congregation will reveal what kinds of people are effectively being reached and those kinds of people who are not effectively being reached. If the dissonance or diversity becomes too much for the recipients to tolerate, they simply vote with their feet and leave the church or never start attending at all. The breadth of that bandwidth is determined by how many frequencies one can broadcast on simultaneously. If a church enlarges its category width and develops an ability to communicate effectively and honor multiple ethnicities simultaneously, then it has the ability to reach a large and diverse audience effectively. Developing that capacity is related to enlarging an organizational-level cultural intelligence.

Earlier, the point was made that urban compression changes the typical social pattern to bring diverse people into close contact with each other. That close contact either drives people into ethnic enclaves—where they huddle with people like themselves in a kind of protective cluster, therefore creating mono-ethnic sanctuaries where familiarity reigns, albeit in restricted fashion—or it forces a new integration. Where it forces integration with the "other," it tends to challenge deeply held, largely unexamined beliefs and either leads to receptivity toward new ideas and forming a new self-identity, or forces one to become more articulate in defending one's position against the alternatives.

Urban, multicultural churches often serve both goals, providing a safe haven where the intrinsic beauty of one's culture is affirmed, while simultaneously helping its members to negotiate interactions with people unlike themselves. Churches such as the Chinese Church of Christ of Los Angeles, First Chinese Baptist Church of Los Angeles, and the Chinese Evangelical Free Church in Monterey Park, California, all represent multi-ethnic churches that conduct worship services in three languages—Mandarin, Cantonese, and English. The language-specific services help urban dwellers feel at home within their language group yet participate in a larger identity around a Chinese ancestry.

Other urban churches that have found themselves located in multi-ethnic neighborhoods have entertained even greater diversity. For example, in the Wilshire Boulevard district of Los Angeles, at least four churches have attempted to serve the diverse populations speaking English, Spanish, and Korean, and three of the four are either currently offering services in Tagalog (Filipino) or are planning to do so.[17] These churches all started as Anglo churches, but as the neighborhoods around them began to change, they intentionally sought to incorporate new peoples into their congregations.

This pattern of urban churches becoming multi-ethnic in order to adapt to their neighborhood may seem to defy McGavran's Homogeneous Unit Principle (see chapter 7). It appears that when a church becomes more heterogeneous and grows, it goes against his principle of church growth. Is it that McGavran's principle, first developed in India, has more explanatory power in rural contexts but fails in the urban soup? In actuality, homogeneity functions as McGavran predicted, but it is a homogeneity of diversity. If homogeneity conjures up images of bland conformity—of stable, predictable values—it probably does not fit the urban context that, by nature, is an arena of colliding images, sounds, smells, and perspectives. But the nature of the urban space is that it is a place of contradictions and competing identities to the point that the urban dweller is never again a single identity that is known by everyone. Rather, in the urban context the individual carries multiple social identities simultaneously. "Growing up in a pluralistic society means never having only a single model for belief, etiquette, politics, musical taste, intellectual pursuit, or family type. City folks are especially prone to harbor different, even conflicting, loyalties, and values simultaneously. It seems incredible that anyone would suggest a homogeneous church in a setting which makes even psychological consistency itself a struggle."[18]

However, if homogeneity is considered from a different perspective, a fresh perspective emerges. If "churches grow best in settings where their values are shared," going back to the previous discussion on bandwidth, we see that churches attract people who respond well to the message being broadcast. [19] If the church is speaking the language of a people in a way that answers their needs and is relevant to their questions, then it will grow. If the message is foreign or unintelligible it will be rejected. It is possible that multi-ethnic, urban churches do grow because they are homogeneous with their neighborhood. That is, they look like and sound like us. They embody the values of cosmopolitan, urbanized people, with all the contradictions and collisions of perspectives that they generate. They grow primarily because the collection of people inside the church look similar to the people outside the church in terms of the many attitudes toward the world they hold in common. For this reason, many urban churches are multi-ethnic, primarily because they mirror the homogeneity of diversity found in the neighborhood, and only secondarily because they hold to theological beliefs about the unity of God's people or are driven by motivations of reconciliation, as important as these might be. Indeed, from personal experience of having worked in midtown Manhattan for several years, Alan can say that it seemed more strange to withdraw into a mono-cultural gathering on Sunday morning than it did to worship with the rainbow of ethnic colors that he worked with on a daily basis outside the church! Thus the Homogeneous Unit Principle is applicable to the city too! But the homogeneity of the city does not relate to ethnicity as much as it relates to the cosmopolitan worldview of urbanites who eclectically choose from a wide variety of perspectives to create an ethos that is not exactly like any of the original, contributing cultures. The nature of cities is that they naturally create a third space (one that is neither identical to the culture of one's parents nor in thorough opposition to it), a space to construct a new identity free from the constraints of traditional expectations.

The city, then, might be the original birthplace of the multi-ethnic church.[20] It was in the city that the multi-ethnic church took shape and prospered. It was the city that prompted the multi-ethnic church to develop the category width to accept those who were different without judgment or correction. Like a collider that smashes atoms, the city is God's supercollider, with the density of population sufficient to smash diverse people together to create free radicals. And it is the city that provides enough free radicals for each to eventually find their way back to each other in sufficient numbers so as to create a multi-ethnic, multicultural church. Interesting thought!

If the city is like a supercollider, it is also like a radio tower. It transmits innovations across broad regions. Whether the thing being transmitted is fashion, a rap song, or an idea, it is carried along by the expansive influence the city exerts. The multi-ethnic church is one of these forms being transmitted. But what was, in the city, a very natural reflection of the local context, now requires greater intentionality and effort to be made manifest in a place not quite as diverse and cosmopolitan. Many more explanations and greater theological justification must be given in those places where the homogeneity of diversity is not as apparent. In rural and suburban areas, the ethnically blended church is as much of an anomaly as a rigidly mono-ethnic church is in the city. That fact should not discourage us from the effort to plant and grow multi-ethnic churches in those places as examples of the unity that is possible in Christ. Rather, the examples and lessons from the urban, multi-ethnic church provide us with the vision and courage to move forward. As such, multi-ethnic churches are a gift to the body of Christ at large. They are points of strategic leverage that God is using to move the church toward the ultimate reconciliation that is coming. They are signs of the coming kingdom that is breaking forth into current reality, a picture of where all of history is moving as we gather someday around the throne, praising the Lamb who was slain. May we be quick to learn the lessons they provide.

PUTTING INSIGHTS TO WORK

1. Have you observed the different patterns of response among ethnic peoples in your community? If so, describe the patterns you have seen.

2. How wide is your own category width when it comes to feeling comfortable in a multi-ethnic or multicultural setting? How wide is your church's category width? Give some examples of how you know.

3. What do you think about the concept of homogeneity of diversity?

RECONCILIATION CHURCHES

The journey toward becoming a multi-ethnic church is different for every church. For many, the driving passion is evangelism. A prime example is Mosaic Church in Little Rock, Arkansas. Pastor Mark DeYmaz states, "Mosaic is not a church focused on racial reconciliation. Rather, we are focused on reconciling men and women to God through faith in Jesus Christ and on reconciling ourselves collectively with the principles and practices of local churches as described in the New Testament."[1] The Evangelical Free Church agrees that a multi-ethnic church must be focused on more than reconciliation among people. An unidentified editor of *EVFC Today* states, "A truly healthy multicultural church won't be focused on reconciliation between ethnicities or ages, genders or socioeconomic groups. No, the focus will be on reconciling men and women to God through faith in Jesus Christ."[2]

As might be expected, however, other multi-ethnic churches are driven by the desire to demonstrate the visible power of God's reconciliation between people representing various ethnicities, or social or economic statuses. For example, one such church states, "We are a Christian community that seeks to intentionally include all races and all cultural backgrounds. Our mission is to embody God's ministry of reconciliation through our practice of worship, devotion, compassion, and justice. We believe that receiving and sharing God's all encompassing love is our greatest challenge and our only hope (2 Cor. 5:11–21)."[3] While this church also desires to see people come to faith in Christ, the passion for reconciliation between people is the driving factor for its existence. Not surprisingly, these types of multi-ethnic churches go by the title of "reconciliation churches."

While there is no organized national movement for reconciliation churches, there is an expanding organic movement that appears to be building momentum. Some denominations or associations of churches have established reconciliation networks or directors of reconciliation to help train existing churches for reconciliation. For example, even though the Evangelical Free Church states that a "truly healthy multicultural church won't be focused on reconciliation between ethnicities or ages, genders or socioeconomic groups," the denomination nevertheless created the position of Director of Reconciliation.[4] A quick search on the Internet reveals that the emphasis on reconciliation spans across all denominations and theological perspectives, from United Methodist, to the Pentecostal/Charismatic Churches of North America, to nearly every church group in the United States.

RECONCILIATION CHURCH MOVEMENT

Even a cursory glance at the history of the United States reveals the regrettable fact that our society has not been kind to minorities. Beginning with the unjust treatment of Native Americans, to the dehumanizing slavery of Africans, to the hatred of Chinese, the sad story of discrimination is heard throughout our national history.

An unfortunate but related aspect of our history of discrimination is the truth that often Christians, and the church at large, ignored the teaching of Scripture for justice. In some cases, church leaders even used Scripture to support racial discrimination. Some Christian voices spoke against injustice. For example, the end of slavery is directly tied to the demands of

Christian people to end the practice, but for far too long, Christian people simply ignored the plight of minorities and the injustices perpetrated upon them.

However, some churches and Christians can be found calling for reconciliation and social justice throughout the entire two-hundred-year history of the United States. For example, during the 1940s and 1950s, evangelists Billy Graham and Oral Roberts both refused to seat people of different races in separate sections. These large evangelistic meetings encouraged people of various ethnicities to sit together, which helped pave the way for churches to focus on reconciliation.

Nationally, the stress on reconciliation took center stage during the civil rights movement of the 1950s. Martin Luther King, Jr.'s calls for justice were couched in biblical terms, and this caused many Christians—mainline and evangelical—to take notice and action. By the1970s, the movement for reconciliation among churches was gaining ground, but it really took hold in the mid-1990s as churches, denominations, and parachurch organizations started focusing seriously on reconciliation. An example of a parachurch organization that raised interest in racial reconciliation in the 1990s is Promise Keepers. Founded in 1990, Promise Keepers purposed to train and teach men how to be godly. The movement quickly gained momentum and around forty-two hundred men attended the first nationwide Promise Keepers conference in 1991. Five years later, the summer conference theme for 1996 was "Break Down the Walls," based on Paul's statement, "For he himself is our peace, who has made the two one and has destroyed the barrier, the dividing wall of hostility" (Eph. 2:14 NIV 84).

The purpose of the conference was to focus men's attention on God's heart for reconciliation. Over a million men attended conferences located at twenty-two stadiums that year. Each conference highlighted speakers of different ethnicities asking for and accepting forgiveness from one another. Men in the audience also expressed guilt for discriminating against one another and were often seen hugging and praying together. The events helped empower the desire for reconciliation churches among many in attendance.

Since the 1990s, an increasing interest in reconciliation has grown across the US. It is impossible to determine exactly how many churches have a mission of reconciliation since there is no official list of reconciliation churches, but a best guess points to around 2 percent of all churches, or eight thousand to ten thousand self-identifying as such. Our research suggests that most churches of this type are found in the southern part of the US, although reconciliation churches are found in all major urban centers.

A GOD OF JUSTICE

Reconciliation churches base their mission on the fact that God is just. A favorite passage often cited is Micah 6:8, which states, "He has told you, O man, what is good; And what does the LORD require of you But to do justice, to love kindness, And to walk humbly with your God?" But that is only one of numerous passages from the Old Testament that demonstrates that justice is dear to God's heart. In Psalm 82, God rebukes those who make unjust judgments saying, "How long will you judge unjustly and show partiality to the wicked? Vindicate the weak and fatherless; Do justice to the afflicted and destitute. Rescue the weak and needy; Deliver *them* out of the hand of the wicked" (82:2–4). God tells his people in Isaiah 1:16–17 to "Wash yourselves, make yourselves clean; Remove the evil of your deeds from My sight. Cease to do evil, Learn to do good; Seek justice, Reprove the ruthless, Defend the orphan, Plead for the widow."

Passages in the New Testament call for God's people to work toward reconciliation. Since we are all new creatures in Christ, and God has reconciled us to himself, "He has committed to us the word of reconciliation. Therefore, we are ambassadors for Christ, as though God were making an appeal through us; we beg you on behalf of Christ, be reconciled to God" (2 Cor. 5:17–20). While this passage speaks primarily regarding reconciliation to God through Christ, leaders of reconciliation churches hear overtones of working toward social justice and reconciliation among all people.

Based on God's reconciling work, reconciliation churches strive to visibly illustrate that there is no superiority or inferiority in Christ. Since all human standing is wiped away in Christ (Gal. 3:28), reconciliation churches seek to wipe away all visible signs of ethnic, economic, or social hierarchy. To the extent that a church has not leveled the playing field for all peoples, to that extent it still needs to be evangelized or changed by the good news of reconciliation.

CHARACTERISTICS OF RECONCILIATION CHURCHES

The desire for reconciliation between people of different cultures has taken on a life of its own in the form of reconciliation churches. It is one of the forms of multi-ethnic churches seen in the United States today. So what are the general characteristics and practices of reconciliation churches? Here is a list of the most common identifiers.

Recognition and Personalization

Building a reconciliation church is often difficult to put into practice. Passion always comes first, but application must come to real terms among real people in real context. The first step is to recognize that there is a problem God wants us to address through a reconciliation church. After that, leaders must personalize the issues implicitly in a local context among people.

Wisdom and Intentionality

The next step is to seek God for wisdom. Church leaders begin by addressing reconciliation issues in their own lives, families, and communities. They engage in prayer regularly, asking God for wisdom and direction. This is followed by intentionally interacting with people of a different ethnicity, particularly to listen and learn.

Truth and Honesty

There is a tendency among some church leaders to ignore history. But leaders of reconciliation churches believe history should be studied and embraced if true justice is to be accomplished. Reconciliation churches draw on theological and historical resources to review past and present injustices. They believe that truth must be found and told regarding social and racial injustice. Thus, history must be understood from the view of the disadvantaged person or people, while respecting all people and culture in the telling. This often opens up areas of pain as history is retold from fresh eyes and perspectives. True reconciliation will not happen without past injustices being recognized and faced, and some level of healing reached. Glossing over past issues does not bring about reconciliation.

Repentance and Apology

One of the striking aspects that led to the renewal of Israel during the time of Nehemiah is called identificational repentance. In his brokenness for Israel's condition, Nehemiah said, "I am praying before You now, day and night, on behalf of the sons of Israel Your servants, confessing the sins of the sons of Israel which we have sinned against You; I and my father's house have sinned" (Neh. 1:6). Nehemiah had not personally sinned, but he identified with the sins of his people—past and present—before God.

In a similar manner, just as Nehemiah confessed the sins of his people before God, all reconciliation churches make some sort of statement of repentance and apology for the sins of their past ancestors or nation. They recognize that to a large extent the church and its people are complicit in the sin of injustice, and admit that, even if they as individuals have not been explicitly involved, they are part of a power structure that embodies systemic injustice in its economic, political, and educational systems, and thus, corporate repentance is a necessary ingredient.

Repentance is made through written statements, ritual services of repentance, and regular public comments in the sermons and announcements of the church. For example, a pastor may comment in a sermon that the church has been complicit in the racism found in the United States. By admitting such a thing, dialogue and conversation is opened up among the members of the congregation so that mutual discussion is allowed to bring understanding and healing over time. Yet this is only a start. If reconciliation stops here it is incomplete.

Action and Involvement

Beginning in their own back yards, reconciliation churches participate in activities and projects that model reconciliation. This involves such things as sharing leadership among people of different ethnic, social, or educational standings. It includes the training and inclusion of all peoples in all levels of ministry. But it also means listening to everyone and incorporating their stories of pain and victory in sermons and in the direction of the church. It also involves taking explicit action in serving the poor, working for racial reconciliation, and expanding political and social efforts to serve those who have suffered injustice. As many actions of the church as possible are employed to model reconciliation between all peoples in the church and community.

Honor and Respect

Effort is made to recognize each people group in the church by highlighting their history, story, and culture, particularly in the worship service. This may take the form of trying to blend something of each people group into the service every week, or by occasionally highlighting a particular culture once a month. Social occasions include food from each culture in abundant supply, while church celebrations incorporate artistic expressions of music, drama, dance, painting, sculpture, and other means to highlight each ethnic group.

Justice and Advantage

Reconciliation churches work to bring about justice and undo disadvantage in their communities, regions, or nations. This often means reconciliation churches do not simply work for symbolic reconciliation but also for practical reconciliation. These churches work to overcome disadvantages in housing, education, employment opportunities, health, welfare, and a number of other areas. Reconciliation churches partner with government organizations, as well as nonprofits, to remedy social injustice while giving voice to the weak and powerless. They not only model reconciliation within the church, but also get involved in campaigning for better reconciliation policies in public policy.

Poor and Disadvantaged

Reconciliation churches emphasize serving the poor. They look to the Old Testament prophets and Scripture, such as Isaiah 58, for their vision of seeking justice, freeing the oppressed, feeding the hungry, and clothing the naked. But they also find support in Christ's words that by serving the poor, they are also serving him (Matt. 25:31–46). To live out this vision, they seek to incarnate Christ by being involved with the poor and serving their needs. Practically, this means churches offer social services such as tutoring, food distribution, housing, and the like. It may also mean that churches relocate to less desirable neighborhoods in order to be closer to the poor. For example, one church we studied devoted one half of its basement for a daily soup kitchen, food pantry, and a thirty-five-man homeless shelter. The church also operates a weekday-tutoring center, and has joined with secular leaders to improve housing for people of all income levels.[5]

Biblically speaking, the number one priority for a disciple of Jesus Christ is not doing social justice. The primary purpose in relation to the world is evangelization. There is no comparison between the two when looking at the Bible. The good news of salvation in Jesus Christ pervades every book of the New Testament. For example, wherever the apostle Paul journeyed, he preached the gospel of salvation in Jesus Christ, and then gathered the new believers into a local church. He did not preach the need for reconciliation between different ethnic peoples, although there was a need for such reconciliation everywhere he preached. Paul knew that social justice was not the gospel, but an outworking of the gospel.

Jesus came into the world to save the lost (Luke 19:10; Mark 10:45). Certainly the poor need assistance, the weak and sick need care, and the hungry need food, but if we take care of all these needs and never share the gospel of salvation with them, our assistance is only temporary. They will still go into eternity without Jesus Christ. This is a serious matter.

The witness of the church is, of course, accomplished through the totality of life, through word and action. But social action alone does not fulfill the Great Commission. Efforts at social justice through reconciliation alone cannot substitute for the preaching of the gospel. Neither Christ nor his apostles set out to reform society as an end in itself. Rather the purpose of good works is to cause nonbelievers to acknowledge God and glorify him (Matt. 5:16; 1 Pet. 2:12; 3:1). Reconciliation churches are one of the models of multi-ethnic churches. However, as reconciliation takes place, these churches must redefine their vision toward evangelism. A vision of reconciliation will not likely empower a church over time.

PUTTING INSIGHTS TO WORK

1. How important is reconciliation for churches today? What is the biblical rationale?

2. Have you observed a reconciliation church or been personally involved in one? If so, do you think moving your current church toward a vision of reconciliation would be a good thing? Why or why not?

3. Do you sense that God has placed, or is placing, a burden on your heart to establish a reconciliation church? What makes you feel this way? What steps do you need to take to move in that direction?

11
TRANSITIONAL CHURCHES

The pastor must want the church to grow and be willing to pay the price for growth.
—C. Peter Wagner

Grace Community is a church in transition. From its founding with twenty-six people in 1955, the church experienced solid numerical growth that peaked at 256 worshipers by its thirtieth anniversary in 1985. Ten years later, church leaders noted in their fortieth annual report that the church had declined 20 percent to an average of 204 worshipers. What they did not expect was the continued rapid decline to only sixty-five worshipers in 2005, the church's fiftieth anniversary. Today, the mostly Anglo congregation of some thirty persons keeps the doors of the church open by renting its facility to two churches—one Korean and the other Hispanic.

An analysis of the church's growth shows a ten-year decline of 68 percent, while the community around the church has grown 15 percent in the same period. Growth of the immediate area within a five-mile radius of the church is projected to increase by about 6 percent in the next five years, but projection for the church is dire. If the church continues on its current slope of descent, it is likely to close some time in the next five to ten years.

Grace Community Church is struggling to respond to a changing neighborhood. When the church was started in the mid-1950s, the community around it was over 95 percent Anglo, with just 5 percent Hispanics. Like numerous other neighborhoods in southern California, the area within a five-mile radius of Grace Community Church has changed significantly. A recent analysis of the ethnic makeup of the church compared to the community showed the following results:

FIGURE 11.1		
Ethnic Diversity	**Grace Community Church**	**Neighborhood**
Hispanic	9 percent	39.7 percent
Black	0 percent	2.5 percent
Asian/Other	13 percent	26.7 percent
Anglo	78 percent	31.1 percent

Obviously, the church no longer reflects the ethnic makeup of its neighborhood. But this is just a small part of a larger problem. Further analysis revealed that the average age of church attendees is fifty, while the average age in the neighborhood is just thirty-four. As can be seen from the statistics below, Grace Community Church does not match the age profile of those in the immediate neighborhood.

FIGURE 11.2		
Ages (years)	**Grace Community Church**	**Neighborhood**
less than twelve	0 percent	18.8 percent
twelve to twenty	6.45 percent	10.9 percent
twenty-one to thirty-four	3.22 percent	19.6 percent
thirty-five to fifty	29 percent	24.1 percent
over fifty	61.29 percent	26.6 percent

The church has a small core of people who support the ministry but, unfortunately, there are numerous danger signs that suggest this is a critical point in the life of the church. The downward momentum in worship attendance will tend to pull the church even further downward. Reversing this steep of a decline is nearly impossible. But reversals have been observed in some situations. The age makeup found in Grace Community Church does not reflect the immediate community within a five-mile radius. The median age of people in the church is sixty-eight, while that of the community is thirty-two. When a discrepancy of this magnitude exists between the people in the church and the local community, it is extremely difficult to attract newcomers.

The attendance at worship will also be a deterrent to attracting new people. Worship auditoriums can be described as uncomfortably empty, comfortably empty, comfortably full, and uncomfortably full. Based on a church's seating capacity of three hundred people, these descriptions would be as follows:

Uncomfortably Empty: Less than one hundred worshipers
Comfortably Empty: Between 101 and 150 worshipers
Comfortably Full: Between 151 and 250 worshipers
Uncomfortably Full: Over 250 worshipers

This means the current worship attendance of thirty-five people is very uncomfortable for new people. The empty auditorium has the effect of making newcomers feel embarrassed and awkward. Add to this the fact that Grace Community Church was founded in 1955 and is now over fifty years old means it is at the end of its healthy life cycle, and major decisions regarding the future of the church need to be faced and made quickly. But the mismatch between the ethnic makeup of Grace Community Church and the people in the community will make it difficult to grow in the future.

The illness facing Grace Community Church is called "ethnikitis." C. Peter Wagner first identified this church disease in the 1970s. He described it as "a terminal illness caused by changing community conditions beyond the control of the local church."[1] During the 1970s, ethnikitis was the number one killer of local churches in the United States. The two major symptoms that were found in churches with ethnikitis were ethnic and socio economic change.

While Grace Community Church still has a chance to renew its ministry, most churches with ethnikitis die. In the 1980s, Gary consulted with a Christian and Missionary Alliance Church in Hawthorne, California, that was suffering from ethnikitis. At the time of the consultation, membership was sixty-three and worship attendance stood at forty-eight persons, but the church had declined 47 percent in the previous decade. The ethnic makeup of the congregation was 93 percent Anglo, but the greater Hawthorne area was only 13 percent Anglo. Hawthorne Alliance Church did not match the people in the community where it was located. The church was like an island surrounded by a sea of different ethnic and socioeconomic people groups. Over time people in the church relocated to other neighborhoods, but some still made the trip back to church on Sunday mornings. Unfortunately, the church was unable to reach people in the immediate church community, and a declining financial base gradually led to cutbacks in ministry. As older members of the congregation found themselves unable to make the commute to church, membership and attendance declined until the church closed its doors. Death by ethnikitis. It was and is a common story for numerous churches.

OPTIONS FOR REVITALIZATION

Wagner labeled ethnikitis a terminal illness due to the challenge of restoring churches with this disease to health and vitality. In the 1970s, ethnikitis was compared to the worst forms of cancer in that, while some people survive cancer, many eventually succumb. However, like with cancer, research throughout the years has led to advances in care and cures. Today there are six possible options that churches with ethnikitis can choose.

Option 1: Close the Church

No one likes to think about closing churches. Yet research has confirmed that around 1 percent of all churches close their doors each year, and transitional churches most likely make up the bulk of them. If a congregation has experienced a decade or more of decline, it is worth asking if the people have the passion and energy to work at revitalizing the church. The following are some key questions to think about. First, do you have a public worship attendance greater than fifty people? Second, do you have more than twenty-five giving units? Third, do you have one leader for every ten people? Fourth, do your existing members have an average tenure less than ten years? Fifth, does your church match its community ethnically and socioeconomically? If you answer "no" to these questions, it indicates your church must make highly significant changes in order to thrive once again. And, in some situations it may even mean it is time to close the doors.[2] Hopefully your church is not in this desperate of a situation and a different option is workable.

Option 2: Continue the Present Ministry to the Dominant Ethnic Group

Most churches begin by tailoring ministry for a specific ethnic group. The style of worship, method of preaching, location of the facility, types of ministries, and a host of other details are all carefully determined to reach a particular people. As the ethnic and socioeconomic composition of a community changes during the years, the ministries of a church become less and less fruitful. When church leaders recognize they are facing the challenge of ethnikitis, they may, and often do, decide to continue church ministry with little change. Leaders who choose this option are essentially deciding to do nothing and die. The potential for revitalization is limited since the program of the church is aimed at a different audience, an audience that no longer lives close enough to be part of the church. In most situations this option leads to the church closing its doors forever.

Option 3: Serve the People in the Immediate Community with Social Programs

A third option that is closely aligned with option 2 is simply to add social programs to serve the new ethnic groups in the community. For example, a church with ethnikitis may continue its ministry unchanged, but begin offering tutorial, educational, or social programs to aid the new people moving into the community. While this is a better option than the second, it often just delays the inevitable. Differences between the church and the new ethnic and socioeconomic groups are often too large to overcome. Church members feel better about themselves, but the end result is usually the same—the church closes.

Option 4: Develop a New Ethnic Church and Give Them the Facility

While many people want to see a multi-ethnic church arise out of ethnikitis, it does not always happen. Sometimes it is best to plant a new mono-ethnic church to reach the new ethnic peoples around the old church. If this option is selected, the following must happen for growth to take place. First, existing members of the church must be educated regarding the realities of ethnic changes going on around them. Second, they must develop a vision and understanding of what it will take to plant a new church among the people God has placed on their doorstep. Third, the church must commit to investing financially in the planting of a new ethnic church. An associate pastor must be hired who is a member of the ethnic group to be reached. All efforts of outreach and assimilation must be directed to the new ethnic group. Fourth, as the new ethnic church grows in size, the Anglo (or other dominant group) must turn over the use of the church's sanctuary or auditorium to them for church services. Of course, the existing church may either merge into the new ethnic group or continue to meet separately in a different room in the church building. Fifth, the existing church donates the old facilities to the new ethnic church and either merges with it, meets in a different room, or leaves to unite with another church. The success potential for this option is determined by the amount of attachment to the facilities and memories of past ministry that members of the older church harbor. If they are unwilling to allow the new church to use the main auditorium or take over the facilities, potential is low. But if the existing people are willing to let go of their memories and control of the facility, potential is high for continued ministry through the new ethnic church.

Option 5: Relocate the Church to a New Site

Perhaps the primary option that transitional churches take is relocation. For many churches this is a wise option to choose, even though it leaves a ministry hole in the community from which the church moves. For relocation to happen, existing members must be willing to part with the current facilities and the memories it contains. It is also important that members be able to establish new patterns of ministry that will effectively reach people in the new community. If a church expects to relocate but continue using the same programs, it is unlikely that the move will be helpful. New communities mean new people and a need for new programs even if the ethnic blend is the same as the existing church members. Existing members must also be able to part with current friends since some people will not make the move. This option is most successful when the church has a senior pastor who has had church planting experience, and who is willing to change the style of ministry to reach the new people in the new location.

Option 6: Develop a Multi-Ethnic Church

One of the best options is to transition into a multi-ethnic church. This strategy is most successful when the senior pastor has significant cross-cultural experience and the congregation has a high desire to demonstrate unity in Christ. The process begins by educating existing church members concerning the changing population trends around the church. Church leaders are educated on missional church growth strategies to enable them to understand what it will take to reach more people in the community.

The target audience to establish a multi-ethnic church is usually second-generation ethnics who feel comfortable being in a complex setting. Thus a church's ministry style is changed to reflect the needs of the people in the community and, quite often, a second pastor is added who represents the ethnic peoples being reached. As quickly as possible, people who are from the new ethnic and/or socioeconomic groups are added to a church's leadership board. For long-term success, diverse leadership must also be added to all subgroups in the church, for example, the ladies' and men's leadership teams, the worship team, as well as youth and children's ministry teams.

TRANSITIONAL CASE STUDY

Rialto Community Baptist Church was organized on January 27, 1957, in Rialto, California. Growth was steady, and by 1966 the church was holding two worship services. Over the ensuing years, several building programs enlarged the church facility to include a six-hundred-seat auditorium, preschool, and kindergarten. Eventually an elementary school was added which grew to over 240 students by 1984.

With the arrival of a new pastor, Rev. Jay Pankratz in 1989, the church began holding services on new property located near the old church facility. Eventually the church built a multipurpose building on the new site and relocated there in March of 1992. The church adopted the new name of Sunrise Church (taken from Luke 1:78–79) in March 1995. Growth continued, and today, Sunrise Church is home to some four thousand people meeting in three different locations.

The church was founded to serve the needs of typical lower- to middle-socioeconomic white Caucasians. By the late 1970s, the community around Rialto, California, was transitioning into a somewhat Hispanic and African-American neighborhood. Most of the new ethnics were upwardly socially mobile, and some of them assimilated into the predominately white Community Baptist Church by the time Pastor Pankratz arrived in 1989.

After his arrival, he crafted a purpose statement that read, "We will seek to reach all ethnic groups without distinction or separation." For the next six years, more nonwhites came to Community Baptist Church, and Pastor Pankratz endured a lot of criticism from those who did not wish to see the new ethnic peoples in the church and from others who did not feel the church was moving fast enough in becoming multi-ethnic. It was a difficult six years, and Pastor Pankratz nearly resigned. But growth took off in the seventh year of Pastor Pankratz's ministry and has continued unabated.[3]

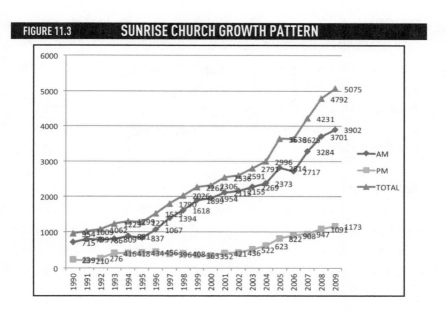

FIGURE 11.3   SUNRISE CHURCH GROWTH PATTERN

By the turn of the century (2000), the church was averaging around two thousand worshipers, which was comprised of about 50 percent Caucasians, 25 percent Hispanics, and 25 percent African-Americans. Sunrise was a heterogeneous church with a solid mix of ethnic people, but it continued to demonstrate a homogeneity by primarily attracting upwardly mobile people of all ethnic groups.

The vision of Sunrise Church today reads:

Our Vision

Our dream at Sunrise Church is to welcome people from all ethnicities, backgrounds, and age groups. As such, by God's grace we will be a multi-ethnic, multi-cultural, and multi-generational church that reaches people for Christ. We will proclaim the good news locally, and in the regions beyond. We will expand our ministry by planting extension churches and reaching those communities for Christ.

Multi-Ethnic

The Bible teaches that God does not discriminate between people of different ethnicities. He welcomes them all into His family as they believe in His Son the Lord Jesus. He also commands His people not to discriminate. As much as possible, the church should resemble heaven. There we find souls "from every nation, tribe, people and language" (Rev. 7:9).

Multi-Cultural

Culture can be defined as "the customary beliefs, social forms, and traits of a particular group." Sunrise Church does not believe that God excludes anyone because of his or her cultural background. His people should also welcome and be enriched by people from different backgrounds.

Multi-Generational

In recent years, we've witnessed some "generational divides." But the Bible instructs us not to divide, rather appreciate one another even though we may represent different age groups (see Titus 2:1–8). Sunrise Church brings people together while recognizing each group's needs.

Multi-Site

In obedience to the Great Commission, Sunrise Church has reached out beyond its own community in order to establish Bible teaching churches that reproduce themselves. As God leads us, we will expand our church to other locations in order to reach those people for Christ.[4]

Sunrise Church continues to see transition. The ethnic makeup of its four thousand plus attendees today is close to 70 percent Hispanic, 20 percent Caucasian, and 10 percent African-American. It stands as one of the best models in the US of a church that was able to transition from a mono-ethnic church to a multi-ethnic one.

TRANSITIONAL PRINCIPLES AND PRACTICES

Observation of effective transitional churches like Sunrise Church points to several common principles and practices.

First, the church is located in a contextual situation that gives support to a multi-ethnic church. It seems almost too obvious to point out, but a multi-ethnic church will only arise from a multi-ethnic community. Church leaders may have a passion for multi-ethnic ministry, but without being in the right community it is not likely to happen.

Second, the senior pastor must have a passion for developing a multi-ethnic church, and the willingness to pay the price to take the church in that direction. Pastors in transitional churches will be misunderstood and will be lightening rods for criticism. They must be willing to endure for at least six to seven years to see real change take place.

Third, a critical mass of existing attendees and lay leaders must support the vision of a multi-ethnic church. In some churches, a small negative core of only 10 percent of the people can cause enough pain that the church cannot move forward. While it varies from church to church and depends a great deal on the policy of governance used by a church, a large enough critical mass must be present to ensure that votes go in the direction of establishing a multi-ethnic church. Some pastors may have the vision for a multi-ethnic church, but without the support of leaders and congregants, it is not likely to happen.

Fourth, if there is a pastoral staff, it must reflect the ethnic blend that the church desires to achieve. For example, if a church hopes to reach Asians, Caucasians, and Hispanics, the pastoral staff must be represented by at least one member of each of these ethnic groups. This holds true for support staff roles, such as secretaries and administrative workers, too.

Fifth, minority members of the congregation must also be well represented on the boards, committees, and ministry teams in the church. It is particularly important that people of representative ethnicities be in highly visible positions, such as members of the worship team, children's workers, greeters, ushers, and parking attendants. This visibility shouts loudly to guests that the church is multi-ethnic.

Sixth, the blending or use of various worship styles in the worship services is another crucial ingredient toward developing a multi-ethnic church. It is helpful if the worship leader or pastor is from a different ethnic group than the preaching pastor. Not only will this present visible evidence that the church is serious about being multi-ethnic, but it will allow for the mixing of differing ethnic blends in the worship service.

All advertising, website, mailers, brochures, and the like must include photos that are multi-ethnic. Anyone looking at such advertising material will naturally conclude that the church is similar to the pictures they view.

Seventh, preaching and teaching from the pulpit and in small groups and classes must include illustrations from different ethnic peoples and contexts. This will mean a lot of extra work for pastors and lay teachers since most of us tend to draw illustrations out of our own ethnic backgrounds. Team teaching by people of different ethnicities may prove to be a real benefit to illustrating messages and teaching in a multi-ethnic church. This will include the use of quotes from well-known ethnic leaders.

Eighth, including stories and testimonials from people of different ethnicities from the pulpit and in classes and small groups will also prove to be an excellent way to demonstrate the multi-ethnic nature of a church.

Ninth, designing evangelistic events, short-term mission trips, and a foreign mission program that encourages worshipers to pray for those of different ethnic backgrounds will build a strong passion for others. Providing opportunities for members to invite their neighbors, family members, and friends to special events and worship services also opens doors of acceptance and understanding.

The exact number is unknown but with the large number of ethnic peoples in the United States, there is no doubt a lot of change going on in countless neighborhoods around the country. As communities experience ethnic and socioeconomic changes, churches of all sizes and denominations are facing a season of transition. It is our hope that most of these churches will be able to make the transition to a multi-ethnic church rather than closing.

PUTTING INSIGHTS TO WORK

1. Is your church in a transitional neighborhood or community? What leads you to say it is or is not? What do you think the future holds regarding the ethnic or socioeconomic changes in the area around your church?

2. Which of the six options for transitional churches do you think is the best one? If your church is in a transitional community, which option would you like your church to adopt? Which one do you think most of your leaders prefer? Your lay members?

3. If your church chose to become a multi-ethnic church, which of the nine principles and practices of transitional churches would pose the largest challenge for your church? Which ones do you think would be the easiest to implement? Why do you think this way?

LEARNING FROM THE MULTI-ETHNIC CHURCH

Each type of church has a different evangelistic potential. In proclaiming the Gospel, each is really issuing a different invitation, since every invitation to follow the Saviour also means "come and be a Christian along with us."
—Donald A. McGavran

Compared to what most pastors have learned in seminary or experienced in their local church, it is clear that the multi-ethnic church has much to teach us. Most seminary education has been rich in biblical and theological studies with some attention to ministry methods, such as preaching, teaching, and counseling. However, most seminaries and pastoral training programs have given little attention to properly understanding the context of ministry. Yet without this element, we become masters of the text of Scripture and amateurs in understanding the context of ministry. Unless we understand both the text and the context we will never serve as good bridges of biblical truth for our day and time. This study on the multi-ethnic church is offered to help us understand what God is doing in the world and how we can cooperate more with him in the process. The lessons that follow capture some of the insights that have emerged thus far in our study.

LESSONS LEARNED

While most of us have a growing awareness that multi-ethnic churches are becoming more common, it is likely that few have understood the driving forces that are making multi-ethnicity a dominant trend for the next decade or two. Some mono-ethnic churches may remain insular and ignorant, but in doing so they will miss many opportunities to reach the unchurched in their own backyard. As we have noted throughout this book, our backyard is really a complex mix of many backyards. The following are some lessons we must take to heart in the United States if we hope to engage in fruitful ministry in the coming decades.

Multi-Ethnic Churches Represent the Next New Trend

When the two forces of rapid urbanization and global migration are considered together, it is apparent that these social forces are now generating, and will continue to generate, a high diversity of peoples, backgrounds, and cultures in the United States, compressing them into high density environments. Cross-cultural interaction, then, is inevitable even in areas of the country previously untouched by these new realities.

In addition to the increasing diversity and density of people unlike the majority population, two other forces are creating conditions where pluralism is on display: television and the Internet. Through this media, a new globalization is taking place that brings divergent opinions and worldviews into the living room. As a result, the average person is more familiar and comfortable with different cultures and perspectives. The former ways of seeing the world only through the eyes of one's own culture are slowly being replaced with a greater tolerance toward those different from us, be they gay, poor, or Hindu. This growing awareness and tolerance is increasingly translated into the church where a growing number of people want to see diversity in attendance, worship, and fellowship. Trends such as these ensure that the multi-ethnic church will be the preferred place of worship for people who desire to see the church look similar to the community around it. Consider this: Why would someone who works, shops, and plays with people of different cultures not desire that same diversity in a church? After a while, the wide variety of people become part of the world in which we live, and little thought is given to creating a separate environment within the church. Diversity becomes the homogeneity that bonds people together (a homogeneity of diversity).

Neither Exclusive, nor Uniform, but Biblically Inclusive

Scripture does not support an ethnic or cultural exclusivism that retreats into an inwardly focused, self-serving existence. Rather, just like Abraham, we have been blessed in order to be a blessing to the nations (Gen. 12:1–3). We are stewards of a great treasure, not to benefit ourselves only, but to share with the multitudes around us. Therefore, we are obligated, even mandated, to welcome the stranger, the foreigner, the widow, and the orphan. We are to provide for their needs, affirm their worth before God, and invite them to the feast God has provided.

In the same way, we are not called to eradicate cultural diversity, to homogenize it into a uniform soup, or to find a neutral form that eliminates all flavor. Rather we are to recognize that the diversity of cultures reflects the creative nature of God in whose image each group of people is created. So in the same way that endangered species are protected or conservation of nature is encouraged, the church must value each cultural expression as a living history of God's work in its midst.

The great lesson that emerges is that the church must be biblically inclusive, seeking to grow in love and respect for people who are different from the majority. Biblical inclusivism does not mean we unilaterally accept everything that comes from outside the church. Nor does this truth necessarily require that mono-ethnic churches be abandoned, or that one's cultural roots be chopped off. What it does mean is that mono-ethnic churches must appreciate and be sensitive to the needs of the minorities. They must be moved with a burden to reach out, to serve, and to welcome the stranger. They must seek to overcome the cultural barriers that separate people, to pray for the well-being of minorities, and to be involved in their lives. In so doing, mono-ethnic churches can move intentionally into a learning posture and a missional heart that places people and their needs over personal preferences and traditional ways of doing things. The minority, or the stranger, must be allowed to point out the blind spots we all have and help us all grow in grace. In short, monocultural or homogeneous churches have an opportunity to become more inclusive, more sensitive, and more intentional in moving toward multi-ethnic engagements that will reveal the great glory of God and the richness of his people.

The importance of planting and growing multi-ethnic churches that offer to the world a picture of the coming kingdom is incalculable. These churches model reconciliation between the races and provide space that allows for mutual understanding and selfless love to develop. They offer to immigrant, urban, or marginalized peoples, who may not fit the conforming expectations of many traditional churches, a place to grow spiritually and relationally; a place to call home.

Multi-Ethnic Churches Are Strategic Points of Investment

Multi-ethnic churches are a gift to the body of Christ. They do so many things better than most traditional homogeneous churches. They represent, then, a strategic model into which the church at large must invest. They form a place of high leverage where many ministry goals can be accomplished simultaneously in ways that are efficient to move the mission of God forward.

In terms of evangelism, multi-ethnic churches are especially effective in several key ways. First, they are highly efficient in reaching multiple ethnicities at once. Rather than establishing a homogeneous church for each ethnic group, the multi-ethnic church brings them all together in one place. The time and effort it would take to assemble a critical mass to form a separate church for each people group is made simpler in the multi-ethnic church where a scale of efficiency is engaged.

Second, multi-ethnic churches are strategic in reaching the nations. History shows that the gospel naturally flows along the lines of relational networks. As immigrant people communicate to extended families back in the motherland, the seeds of the gospel are planted. Some multi-ethnic churches have extended their influence internationally through this means.

Third, multi-ethnic churches help in identifying and reaching receptive people. Donald McGavran, George Hunter, and others have provided insights in how to find and minister to receptive people in whom God has already been at work.[1] Ethnic peoples, especially recent arrivals, represent those most prepared to receive the gospel if we have the eyes to see them. For example, Hunter points out that people experiencing major culture change, have recently moved to a new place, or are experiencing important life transitions are generally more receptive to the gospel than the average person. The multi-ethnic church naturally draws immigrant and marginalized people who have recently moved, and are undergoing transition. These people are generally more open to new ideas including the gospel message.

Fourth, multi-ethnic churches are excellent for creating a third place. The founder of Starbuck's wanted to create a third place that was not home and not work but represented a place where people could get together and hang out over a cup of coffee. To do that, he made Wi-Fi available with comfortable chairs and tables which encouraged people to hang out for longer periods of time to fellowship. In effect, in addition to selling coffee, he created a sense of community. In a similar manner, the multi-ethnic church breaks down the polarity of us (our kind) and them (their kind), and creates unique spaces for the cultures to come together and learn from each other. Multi-ethnic churches help us broaden our category width and learn to think in new and innovative ways. They stretch our CQ, our cultural intelligence. As a result they represent a real gift to the church at large.

Finally, in addition to stretching our cultural intelligence, multi-ethnic churches also help us as individuals, churches, and denominations to see our blind spots and cultural assumptions that we often take for granted. The old saying "It wasn't a fish that discovered water" applies to most of our ethnocentric monoculturalism. We do not know what we do not know. It is hard for us to see our own mistaken or limited ways of thinking. Multi-ethnic churches expose our assumptions and teach us humility and grace. The genius of the multi-ethnic church is that it challenges us all to aspire to higher values.

Multi-Ethnic Churches Require Much Effort to Lead

Emerging from the research is the realization that multi-ethnic churches are a challenge to lead and manage. Whereas most churches do not think much about culture and worldview, in the multi-ethnic church cultural factors loom large. Differing languages, cultural assumptions, communication patterns, ways of handling conflict, leadership styles, and behavioral codes all create a complex soup that can frustrate and confuse leaders. Pastors who rise to this challenge often have prior cross-cultural experience, display an unusual capacity for situational leadership, and are deeply committed to theological convictions that drive them to engage this difficult leadership challenge. Maintaining balance in the congregation while ministering to the changing needs of diverse groups is trying for the best leaders. For these reasons, much more research is needed in order to resource and support leaders who are on the front lines of ministry innovations.

RESPONDING TO THE MULTI-ETHNIC CHALLENGE

Summarizing lessons learned helps consolidate concepts and clarify thinking. But to bring the most benefit to the church in both its homogeneous and heterogeneous expressions, some resolutions for future action need to be adopted. The following are suggested next steps to improve our understanding and service in a multicultural world.

For Individuals

The corporate strength of a church in the area of cultural intelligence is related to the level of the cultural intelligence of individuals within it. While much can be done to prepare the church to become more welcoming to those of other ethnicities, one's personal responsibility in this matter cannot be shirked. A careful study of Scripture reveals God's intention that the gospel be made available to the nations, both near and far. As citizens of God's kingdom, we must grow in our ability to share the good news, as well as our lives, with those who are different from us. How do we learn to do this? What practices are helpful? David Livermore, in his book *Cultural Intelligence: Improving Your CQ to Engage Our Multicultural World*, offers practical suggestions in this regard:

- Read books written by people of other cultural perspectives.
- Watch films, including foreign films, to broaden our perspective.
- Go to ethnic restaurants and learn the culture behind the food.
- Journal and become more aware of our surroundings.
- Learn a new language.
- Attend cultural celebrations and ask for help understanding what we see.
- Go to the mosque or Pride Parade to encounter beliefs with which we conflict.
- Be informed about the world beyond our borders.
- Look for what is behind the actions, words, or art when you are with those unlike us.
- Study the Scripture with people from other contexts.
- Do mission with and not only to the oppressed and disadvantaged.
- Beware of culturally embedded language.
- Speak slowly and be patient when talking with others who do not quickly understand us.
- Observe body language and pay attention to what is being communicated nonverbally by ourselves and others.
- Imitate behaviors of those we are learning about.
- Find a cultural guide, an insider who is willing to explain his or her culture.
- Take a course to understand culture and people.
- Serve in a ministry project with an ethnically diverse group of people.
- Travel to a different culture and get away from the Westerners. Go deep.
- Attend a wedding ceremony or other kind of ceremony of someone from a different culture.

- Read the local paper when traveling, not *USA Today*.
- Walk through the grocery store of an ethnic group.
- Seek out and spend time with those who are different.
- Always ask questions, listen hard! [2]

These are some ways we can begin to work now to expand our cultural intelligence and develop greater category width. We can determine to become a bridge to bring the cultures together. In this way, we show respect and honor for those who are different. Remember how much Christ did to reach into our world!

For Pastors

Assess the Number and Types of Ministry Gatherings. As noted in a previous chapter, most multi-ethnic churches, including most mono-ethnic churches, have a mix of homogeneous and heterogeneous groups or gatherings that meet on a regular time schedule. These groupings tend to serve different social functions for those who participate. Homogeneous groups attract like-minded people on the basis of affinity. Birds of a feather do flock together. However, heterogeneous groups combine people with others not like themselves. For most churches, the worship service does this by combining the rich and the poor, the educated and the uneducated, the old and the young, as well as those of different ethnicities. Heterogeneous groupings expose people to new opportunities, new ways of thinking, new affiliations, new responsibilities, and produce better problem-solving skills.[3] Homogeneous groups work best for evangelism and assimilation of newcomers. They work to build strong alliances and help affirm values and group orientation. Auditing our congregations for the number and type of these groups can help those in leadership pinpoint areas of neglect. For example, are there sufficient heterogeneous groupings available for all age groups or are some segments of the congregation under-stimulated by diversity? Conversely, are sufficient numbers of homogeneous groups available as ports of entry for those suffering from transition stress? Careful thinking about the social architecture of the congregation can help church leaders determine the next steps and the most effective action for the future.

Expand Congregational CQ. Pastors of both mono-ethnic and multi-ethnic churches must work to expand their congregation's cultural intelligence. Because the power of culture to shape the way we think and act is so powerful, we have an almost universal need to learn how to expand our cultural sensitivities, our cultural intelligence. More and more, even in the average suburb in the United States, pastors need cross-cultural ministry skills just to serve the people God is bringing into the church! To do this, pastors need to think through how they are exposing their people to different cultural forms and expanding their fluency in cross-cultural engagement.

Furthermore, pastors need to do fresh thinking in:

- Preaching: How can pastors communicate the gospel in ways that make sense to an audience composed of various cultural perspectives? Not only must the content be shaped to speak to multiple cultures, but the ways that message is delivered needs reevaluation as well.
- Worship: How can the worship music and liturgy be shaped to relate to the various cultural traditions of the congregation? Should a church adopt a blended service format, hold multiple services each shaped to a portion of the audience, or rotate musical teams and worship leaders from Sunday to Sunday?
- Evangelism: How should evangelism strategies be focused to reach a particular ethnicity or people group? Once a person comes to Christ, how should he or she be followed up and discipled?
- Conflict Resolution: How can the elders and church leaders be trained to respond to conflict? What conflict resolution styles need to be employed with which group? How can trust be built between groups to help mitigate against destructive conflict erupting?
- Leadership: How should lay leaders and professional staff teams be composed to reflect the diversity of the congregation? How can minority leaders be identified early and equipped to lead their

communities? What leadership styles need to be employed that respect the cultural backgrounds of the diverse people in the church?

Auditing both the number and type of groups in the church (heterogeneous and homogeneous), as well as each of the church's ministry systems for their cross-cultural utility is critical. Such an audit will reveal weaknesses and allow the ministry team to make the necessary preparations to move the church toward more robust multi-ethnic ministry.

For Denominations and Seminaries

If individuals, pastors, and churches are to take concrete steps to be more sensitive to multi-ethnic issues, it should also be the goal of denominations, seminaries, and Bible colleges. To respond to our rapidly changing world we need to carefully review our equipping tracks for pastors, as well as the way we serve our churches. The following suggestions are offered with the goal to prompt new thinking on the macro scale.

Bible college and seminary curriculum is mostly focused on equipping in the area of biblical and theological studies (exegeting the text) with some attention to pastoral methods. However, very few pastoral candidates are equipped to exegete the context of ministry. Often the assumption is made that the ministry context of one's own country and culture is already understood, so little attention needs to be given to further community analysis. Unfortunately, nothing could be further from the truth. Ministry contexts are constantly changing. Neighborhood demographics are constantly in flux. The world of the church is becoming further removed from the world of everyone else.

Perhaps one of the greatest gifts a missionary can receive is the inability to speak in the language of his newly adopted people. Consequently, he must slow down, often for a period of years, and laboriously learn the culture, history, and language of the people to whom he is sent. Unfortunately, in our own home countries we rush right past these steps, assuming we already know what the people in the area need to hear and how they need to hear it.

To help meet this challenge, schools and denominational offices need to develop and make available (through formal, informal, and nonformal education) training in the following areas:

Cross-Cultural Competence. Classes, seminars, and personalized coaching should be focused on equipping pastors and lay ministry leaders in terms of how to understand the context of ministry, including the tools and perspectives for learning about the people groups that make up the populations in the ministry area.

Leading Change. Installing major changes in an existing church can be a perilous endeavor in any case, but when the changes proposed relate to the core identity of the congregation and are as complex as blending different cultures, the stakes increase. Careful thought and coaching should be given to any pastor seeking to transition an existing church toward multi-ethnicity. Such skills are necessary as well for new seminary graduates who wish to plant multi-ethnic churches. Even when the church is newly planted, it is likely the pastor will need to coach believers who have no cross-cultural skills on how to do ministry in a different way.

Conflict Resolution. Skills in biblically informed conflict resolution is a must for ministry, but even more so in a multi-ethnic church where the potential for misunderstanding is multiplied. Leaders of multi-ethnic churches need training to preemptively head off conflict before it becomes destructive. Such training needs to speak to interpersonal conflict resolution skills, as well as stewarding conflict on a corporate level. Special attention should be given to understanding how cultural patterns relate to conflict resolution as well.

Consider Region-Wide Strategies. On the macro level, denominational or seminary leadership should scan the region to identify successful multi-ethnic churches that can serve as living case studies for church leaders. Churches that have a track record for managing the complex dynamics of multi-ethnic churches can become laboratories for those contemplating such a ministry. However, many multi-ethnic churches are so involved in running the church's ministries that they give little thought for passing on their knowledge and expertise. These churches need denominational or seminary assistance to tell their story and share their best practices to empower a movement of like-minded ministries. Here the seminary can provide a valuable service by networking churches together.

Offer Study Scholarships to Emerging Minority Leaders. In order to fast-track emerging minority leaders into positions of fruitful service, denominations and seminaries should offer advanced educational opportunities with the explicit purpose of placing minority leaders into local church and regional ministries. Specifically partnering with multi-ethnic churches will help identify and empower these leaders.

Link Congregations for Greater Partnership

Forging connections between mono-ethnic and multi-ethnic churches offers strategic advantages to both types of churches. At times, a mono-ethnic church homogeneously related to a selected target population may provide the best place for a new believer or new immigrant family to be located, so as to offer a safe place to land. In the same way, mono-ethnic churches can refer their members or converts who would profit from a blended congregational experience to multi-ethnic churches. The exchange of members and resources can potentially help both churches succeed in their ministry effectiveness.

PRINCIPLES FOR LEADING MULTI-ETHNIC CHURCHES

We are excited about what God is doing in the United States in both mono-ethnic and multi-ethnic churches. To us, it appears that God is stirring up his church to engage our changing cultures with the powerful gospel of salvation in Jesus Christ alone. Note that we say cultures (plural) rather than culture (singular). The United States is no longer a single, monolithic culture; in fact it never really has been. In practical terms, the great diversity of peoples, cultures, and worldviews necessitate the establishment of all kinds, styles, and sizes of local churches to reach the vast mosaic we call the United States. One church—no matter its form—will not be able to reach everyone. Diversity of peoples demands diversity of churches.

The gathering of many different peoples into our urban centers is birthing multi-ethnic churches of various types. However, there are some common practices, or principles, that all multi-ethnic churches employ. The following are a few we have observed.

Inclusive Worship

It should be obvious at this point that there are many right ways to worship. Assuming that worship is biblically and theologically sound, what is right depends on the people one is seeking to reach with the gospel. To reach first-generation Koreans, right worship usually means preaching and singing in Korean. If one is reaching second-generation Japanese, however, right worship most often means preaching and singing in English.

Right worship in a multi-ethnic context must include some degree of cultural blend, but goes far beyond that to include culturally appropriate communication, such as storytelling, preaching, level of emotion, and the like.

Diverse Leadership

Everything rises and falls on leadership, and it is no different in multi-ethnic churches. One ingredient that every successful multi-ethnic church has is a leader who is passionate about the church. Indeed, we believe that no multi-ethnic church will exist or survive for long without a leader who is passionate about building a multi-ethnic church. This suggests an inherent danger regarding the long-term nature of multi-ethnic churches. When the founding pastors leave, as they all do eventually, it is predictably difficult to replace them with another pastor who has the same passion. Therefore, some multi-ethnic churches likely will become more homogeneous over time as new senior pastors are appointed or called to ministry.

The leadership teams, pastoral staff, governing board, and ministry teams, must reflect the ethnic diversity found in the congregation. Of particular importance are the people visible on the platform during worship and general meetings. The visibility of pastors and worship leaders communicates a great deal about the church's values. Diversity of leadership communicates that the church is serious about sharing power with all ethnic groups in the church.

Of course, the sharing of leadership among those of different people groups is what brings true cultural blending and discovery to bear on the ministries of the church. As leaders representing the different ethnic cultures work together, elements of each culture become embedded into the ministry structure at subconscious levels, making for a true multi-ethnic church.

Kingdom Attitudes

The gathering of different ethnic groups creates the opportunity for strong passions to ignite. No multi-ethnic church lasts for a long time unless the leaders and congregants commit to living out kingdom attitudes such as loving one another, preferring others over themselves, and being willing to be last so others can be first.

Other attitudes are just as important. For example, an attitude of flexibility allows members to adapt in numerous ways. If congregants are not willing to flex, it is doubtful a multi-ethnic environment can be established, or at least maintained for long. An attitude of intentionality is also a must in multi-ethnic churches. For the most part, if leaders do not intentionally work to build a multi-ethnic church, it will not happen. It takes deliberate thought and effort to see a multi-ethnic church built.

Right Context

Multi-ethnic churches are empowered by their surrounding context. It is obvious that a church located in a community that is comprised of one ethnic group will not be highly diverse. That is why most multi-ethnic churches are found in urban centers of the United States. Some smaller communities do have enough ethnic and economic diversity to allow for some multi-ethnic churches to exist, but the context is key.

Research Gary conducted over the last decade with over one thousand church visitors discovered that 91 percent lived within twenty miles of the church they attended. This ministry area is predictable wherever churches are located, that is, cities or rural areas. The one exception was among ethnic groups with high people consciousness. Among those groups, individuals often traveled as much as two hours to gather with others like themselves.

Thus, 90 percent of churches in the United States should focus on designing ministry to reach those within a twenty-minute or twenty-mile drive from their place of worship. If the community is highly diverse, the church may have the opportunity to become multi-ethnic. But if the community is homogeneous, the church should focus on reaching the mono-ethnic peoples who reside there. Jesus set the agenda in the Great Commission, but it must be played out in the real contexts of our backyards.

Manage Challenges

Pastors and other leaders in multi-ethnic churches are able to manage the following major challenges.

- The challenge of communicating a theology and philosophy of multi-ethnic ministry that gains ownership among the members of the congregation.
- The challenge of including representatives of all ethnic peoples in all tiers of leadership throughout the church.
- The challenge of including aspects of all ethnic peoples in the overall ministry of the church.
- The challenge of establishing a governance process and policies that fit the complex cultural makeup of the congregation.
- The challenge of distributing resources equally among all ethnic groups.
- The challenge of coordinating the use of facilities in a spirit of collaboration among all ethnic groups.
- The challenge of training the entire congregation to raise the level of cultural intelligence.
- The challenge of coexisting with speakers of different languages in the same congregation.

These are the major challenges that church leaders face when starting to build a multi-ethnic church, and they must be managed well for a multi-ethnic church to thrive and survive.

Welcoming Hospitality

The way churches welcome newcomers is an important issue for all churches, but it is huge in the multi-ethnic church. The multi-ethnic church promises a great deal to those who listen to its passionate statement about fellowship together. Thus, if it does not provide a hospitable atmosphere, guests will be greatly disappointed and perhaps never make another effort to attend.

Hospitality must be expressed through the greeting practices, music, foods, worship styles, comments, expressions of welcome, and people of the church. Hospitality in multi-ethnic churches goes way beyond a handshake as one walks in the door. Welcoming the strangers in a multi-ethnic church includes the entire church package—what the guest sees, hears, feels, smells, and senses in the experience of attendance. It begins in the parking lot, but continues into the weeks following. Church leaders must think through the entire welcoming process and procedures in a multi-ethnic church. The promise of acceptance and inclusiveness must be met, or the church will not survive being multi-ethnic.

The dream of multi-ethnic churches is becoming a reality today. It is a trend that is not likely to go away in the coming years, nor should it. God is glorified in many ways, but clearly one of the best is when people love one another as Christ loved. In responding to the changing multicultural context, every level of church ministry needs to be engaged: individual, pastoral, corporate, and regional, each working in concert with the greater vision of reaching those who God has placed in the church's orbit. May we move forward in faith and obedience to seize these opportunities that God has offered to us.

PUTTING INSIGHTS TO WORK

1. What lessons have you learned about multi-ethnic churches from reading this book? Do you agree or disagree with the ones mentioned in this chapter?

2. Which of the recommendations resonate the strongest in your mind and heart? Why?

3. What four or five insights regarding multi-ethnic churches are you going to put into practice this year? Name them and explain why they are important to you and your ministry.

Chapter 1

1. Judy Keen, "More Diverse from the Bottom Up," *USA Today*, March 17, 2011.

2. Ibid.

3. Melanie Eversley, "In a First, Hispanics Outnumber Whites," *USA Today*, March 17, 2011.

4. John A. Meyer, "A Letter from the Publisher," *TIME*, July 8, 1985, 3.

5. James R. Gaines, "From the Managing Editor," *TIME*, Fall 1993, 2.

6. Ralph Winter, "Reaching the 'Moving Target,'" *Christianity Today*, July 12, 1985, 18.

7. "Growth of a Nation," *MissionsUSA*, January/February 1986, 61.

8. This definition of missiology is adapted from Alan Tippett, *Introduction to Missiology* (Pasadena, Calif.: William Carey Library, 1987), xiii.

9. Ibid., xix.

10. Joel Kotin, "Ready Set Grow," *Smithsonian*, July/August 2010, 61.

Chapter 2

1. See Joseph L. Graves, Jr., *The Race Myth: Why We Pretend Race Exists in America* (New York: Plume, 2005); and Thomas Sowell, *Race and Culture: A World View* (New York: BasicBooks, 1994).

2. L. Luca Cavalli-Sforza, Paolo Menozzi, and Alberto Piazza, *The History and Geography of Human Genes* (Princeton: Princeton University Press, 1994).

3. For example, many nations do not recognize Taiwan as being an independent nation though it functions as such. However, the Vatican is considered an independent nation, but many people don't think of it in those terms.

4. Ralph Winter was standing on the shoulders of Donald McGavran, who earlier described how the gospel spreads along the family, clan, and tribal lines of people groups. See Donald A. McGavran, *The Bridges of God: A Study in the Strategy of Missions* (Eugene, Ore.: Wipf & Stock, 2005) and *Understanding Church Growth* (Grand Rapids, Mich.: Eerdmans, 1970).

5. According to the 2010 Joshua Project, of these 17,500 people groups, 9,802 of these are described as peoples-across-countries (migrant or dispersed peoples), of which 4,074 were listed as unreached. See Rick Wood, "Reaching Peoples," *Mission Frontiers*, May/June 2010, 5.

6. The US Census Bureau uses categories such as "Latino or Hispanic" interchangeably and by that term consolidates many ethnic identities under a single term around which there is broad agreement.

7. Postmodern universalism asserts that all religions and faiths are only local theological constructs and have no universal claim on all peoples. They may, however, be equally valid or useful in securing eternal life as each faith pursues God as they know him. God will then accept them if they were faithful to their faith. This view is, of course, incompatible with the revelation that Jesus is the only way to the Father as espoused by evangelicals.

8. Ken Davis, "Multicultural Church Planting Models," *The Journal of Ministry and Theology* (Spring 2003): 114–127.

9. Mark Chaves, *National Congregations Study* (Tucson: University of Arizona, 1998). See also National Congregations Study, accessed November 22, 2011, http://www.soc.duke.edu/natcong/.

10. Mark DeYmaz and Harry Li, *Ethnic Blends: Mixing Diversity into Your Local Church* (Grand Rapids, Mich.: Zondervan, 2010), 128.

11. Paul Hiebert quoted by Manuel Ortiz in *One New People: Models for Developing a Multiethnic Church* (Downers Grove, Ill.: InterVarsity, 1996), 149.

12. Dirke D. Johnson, "Multicultural and Racial Reconciliation Efforts Fail to Attract Many in the Black Church," *Great Commission Research Journal*, vol. 2., no. 2 (Winter 2011): 225–226.

13. Charles Gilmer, *A Cry of Hope, A Call to Action: Unleashing the Next Generation of Black Christian Leaders* (Lake Mary, Fla.: Creation House Publishers, 2009), 87–90.

14. R. A. Schermerhorn, *Comparative Ethnic Relations: A Framework for Theory and Research* (Chicago: University of Chicago Press, 1979), 60.

15. Elizabeth Drury, "Leading the Multiethnic Church: Help From New Metaphors and The Leadership Challenge," *Great Commission Research Journal*, vol. 2, no. 2, 205–220.

16. Ibid., 208–209.

17. Ibid., adapted from information provided.

18. Drury also mentions a sixth type, that of the patient church, in which an established church takes on another fledgling church for a specific period of time, giving them encouragement, financial assistance, and space until they are able to stand on their own, move out, and establish their own successful ministries somewhere else.

19. Johnson, 227.

20. Arturo Lucero and Robert R. Weaver, "Building Healthy Relationships in a Multi-Ethnic Congregation with No Ethnic Majority," *Great Commission Research Journal* (Winter 2011): 175–195.

21. Johnson, 223.

Chapter 3

1. Bruce W. Fong, *Racial Equality in the Church: A Critique of the Homogeneous Unit Principle in Light of a Practical Theology Perspective* (Lanham, Md.: University Press of America, 1996), 151.

2. Mark DeYmaz and Harry Li, *Ethnic Blends: Mixing Diversity into Your Local Church* (Grand Rapids, Mich.: Zondervan, 2010), 78.

3. Dirke D. Johnson, "Multicultural and Racial Reconciliation Efforts Fail to Attract Many in the Black Church," *Great Commission Research Journal*, vol. 2, no. 2 (Winter 2011): 225.

4. Miriam Adeney, "Is God Colorblind or Colorful?" *Mission Frontiers* (May/June 2010): 12.

5. We have chosen the term *multiculturalism* here. That is different from multi-ethnic as described before. It seems that God was more interested in the people of Israel to keep a single-minded obedience to him and what he was doing among them. So while it seems the people of Israel were not to adopt the customs and religions of the surrounding nations, they nevertheless were to welcome the foreigner among them as we will see later.

6. Johnson, 229.

7. Arthur F. Glasser, *Announcing the Kingdom: The Story of God's Mission in the Bible* (Grand Rapids, Mich.: Baker Academic, 2003), 59.

8. Ibid., 87.

9. Ibid.

10. The book of Acts records examples of when the church was reluctant to take the gospel across the cultural barriers, and an act of the Holy Spirit did it by causing the apostles to speak in tongues (Acts 2) or scattering the believers through persecution (Acts 8).

11. Johnson, 229.

Chapter 4

1. "2009 Global Trends: Refugees, Asylum-Seekers, Returnees, Internally Displaced and Stateless Persons," Division of Programme Support and Management, UNHCR: The UN Refugee Agency, June 15, 2010, http://www.unhcr.org/ 4c11f0be9.html.

2. Raymond J. Bakke, "Evangelization of the World's Cities," in *An Urban World: Churches Face the Future*, eds. Larry L. Rose and C. Kirk Hadaway (Nashville: Broadman, 1984), 91.

3. "Human Population: Urbanization," Population Reference Bureau, accessed April 3, 2011, http://www.prb.org/Educators/TeachersGuides/HumanPopulation/Urbanization.aspx.

4. "Our Mobile Hemisphere," *Americas Quarterly* (Summer 2008): 64–65.

5. Donald A. McGavran, *Understanding Church Growth* (Grand Rapids, Mich.: Eerdmans, 1970), 281.

6. Ibid., 180.

7. Roger Greenway, quoted by Donald McGavran, *Momentous Decisions in Missions Today* (Grand Rapids, Mich.: Baker, 1984), 179.

8. Charles Van Engen, "Biblical Perspectives on the Role of Immigrants in God's Mission." Paper presented to the Lausanne Theology Working Group, Panama, January 2009, 3.

9. Rachel Zoll, "Megachurches Lauded for Desegrated Services," *The Californian*, February 23, 2007, D–6.

Chapter 5

1. Haya El Nasser and Paul Overberg, "Diversity Grows as Majority Dwindles: Minorities Make up Almost Half of Births," *USA Today*, June 11–13, 2010, 1A.

2. Aaron Claverie, "It's a Boy: Son of Pakistani Immigrants Is Southwest County's First Baby" *The Californian*, January 2, 2009, A–1.

3. Howard G. Hageman, *Lily Among the Thorns* (Grand Rapids, Mich.: Half Moon Press, 1956), 58.

4. "Willing to Be Uncomfortable," *EFCA Today* 84, no. 1 (Spring 2010): 11.

5. Tetsunao Yamamori, "Finding Ethnic America," in *The Pastor's Church Growth Handbook: Volume 1*, ed. Win Arn (Pasadena, Calif.: Church Growth Press, 1979), 182.

6. Ibid., for original study.

Chapter 6

1. Personal, on-site interviews with pastoral staff, June 7, 2011.

2. Not long ago Saddleback hosted at its Lake Forest site: (1) a boomer service for Caucasian audiences in their forties, fifties, and sixties; (2) a traditional service that catered more to senior citizens; (3) a service featuring contemporary rock style worship targeting those in their twenties and thirties; (4) a gospel choir service aimed more at urban and African-American people; and (5) a Hawaiian service using Hawaiian-style worship music. While some of these forms target different ethnicities, most were geared toward serving the various generations and musical preferences of its members.

3. Keith Watkins, "Multi-Language Congregations: A Field Study in Los Angeles 1993," accessed August 25, 2011, http://www.cts.edu/images/encounter/552kwatkins.pdf?ml=4&mlt=system&tmpl=component (site discontinued).

4. Mark DeYmaz and Harry Li, *Ethnic Blends: Mixing Diversity into Your Local Church* (Grand Rapids, Mich.: Zondervan, 2010), 77.

5. Ibid., 130–132. In this description they reference a taxonomy developed by Ed Lee, pastor of Mosaic Community Covenant Church in Sugar Land, Texas.

6. Research had already indicated that minority group members attending multi-ethnic churches with a racial majority tended to have more friends outside the church than majority group members, and their rates for leaving the church were higher. Source: Arturo Lucero and Robert R. Weaver, "Building Healthy Relationships in a Multi-Ethnic Congregation with No Ethnic Majority," *Great Commission Research Journal* (Winter 2011): 175–195.

Chapter 7

1. The Phrase Finder, accessed June 16, 2011, http://www.phrases.org.uk/meanings/birds-of-a-feather-flock-together.html.

2. See Samuel Escobar, "Solicited Comments" in Frederick W. Norris, "The Social Status of Early Christianity," *Gospel in Context* 2, no. 1 (January 1979).

3. For a description and discussion of some critics, see Walther A. Olsen, "The Homogeneous Unit Principle Revisited: Part One," *Journal of The American Society for Church Growth* 8, no. 1 (Spring 1997): 3–16.

4. Reggie McNeal, *The Present Future: Six Tough Questions for the Church* (San Francisco: Jossey-Bass, 2003), 20.

5. Soong-Chan Rah, *The Next Evangelicalism: Freeing the Church from Western Cultural Captivity* (Downers Grove, Ill.: InterVarsity, 2009), 84.

6. Olsen, 14.

7. Donald McGavran, *Understanding Church Growth*, 3rd ed. (Grand Rapids, Mich.: Eerdmans, 1990), 81.

8. Ibid., 69–70.

9. Ibid., 163.

10. One example of an extreme view of the Homogeneous Unit Principle is Rah's *The Next Evangelicalism.*

11. McGavran, 155.

12. Ibid.

13. Merrill C. Tenney, *John: The Gospel of Belief* (Grand Rapids, Mich.: Eerdmans, 1976), 248.

14. Peter T. O'Brien, *Colossians, Philemon*, vol. 44, Word Biblical Commentary (Nashville: Thomas Nelson, 1982), 192.

15. Olsen, 15–16.

16. Ibid., 16.

17. Ibid., part 2, *Journal of the American Society for Church Growth* 8 (Fall 1977): 22.

18. Ibid., 24.

Chapter 8

1. "Migration in an Interconnected World: New Directions for Action," *Report of the Global Commission on International Migration* (Switzerland: SRO-Kundig, 2005), 1.

2. "World Migration Report 2010, The Future of Migration: Building Capacities for Change," IOM International Organization for Migration (Geneva, Switzerland, 2010), 3.

3. "International Migration Report 2006: A Global Assessment," United Nations, Department of Economic and Social Affairs, xv.

4. "Migration in an Interconnected World," 85.

5. "International Migration Report 2006," 1.

6. United Nations Development Program, 2004.

7. "The Newest New Yorkers, 2000," New York City Department of City Planning, Population Division, accessed March 10, 2011, http://www.nyc.gov/html/dcp/html/census/nny_exec_sum.shtml.

8. Sam Roberts, "Listening to (and Saving) the World's Languages," *The New York Times*, April 28, 2010, http://www.nytimes.com/2010/04/29/nyregion/29lost.html?pagewanted=all.

9. "City Basics," April 12, 2005, Lacity.org., accessed April 13, 2010.

10. Personal correspondence, March 17, 2011.

11. The influence of grandparents and other extended family members upon the children as they provide child-care support cannot be under-estimated either.

12. James Lull, *Media, Communication, Culture: A Global Approach*, 2nd ed. (New York: Columbia University Press, 2000), 242–245.

13. Dirke D. Johnson, "Multicultural and Racial Reconciliation Efforts Fail to Attract Many in the Black Church," *Great Commission Research Journal*, vol. 2, no. 2 (Winter 2011): 225–226.

14. Mary C. Waters and Tomas R. Jimenez, "Assessing Immigrant Assimilation: New Empirical and Theoretical Challenges," *Annual Review of Sociology*, Social Science Module 31 (Spring 2005): 107–111.

15. Ibid., 108.

16. Ibid., 108–109.

17. Ibid., 110.

18. Ibid.

19. Prema Kurien, "Becoming American by Becoming Hindu: Indian Americans Take Their Place at the Multicultural Table," in *Gatherings in the Diaspora: Religious Communities and the New Immigration*, eds. R. Stephen Warner and Judith G. Wittner (Philadelphia: Temple University Press), 61–65.

Chapter 9

1. United Nations, *World Urbanization Prospects: The 2007 Revision*, (Department of Economic and Social Affairs, March 10, 2010), 1–2.

2. "Migration in an Interconnected World: New Directions for Action," *Report of the Global Commission on International Migration* (Switzerland: SRO-Kundig, 2005), 1.

3. "World Migration Report 2010, The Future of Migration: Building Capacities for Change," IOM International Organization for Migration (Geneva, Switzerland, 2010), 3.

4. "International Migration Report 2006: A Global Assessment," United Nations, Department of Economic and Social Affairs, xv.

5. United Nations Development Program, 2004.

6. "The Newest New Yorkers, 2000," New York City Department of City Planning, Population Division, accessed March 10, 2011, http://www.nyc.gov/html/dcp/html/census/nny_exec_sum.shtml.

7. Sam Roberts, "Listening to (and Saving) the World's Languages," *The New York Times*, April 28, 2010, http://www.nytimes.com/2010/04/29/wanted=all.

8. "City Basics," April 12, 2005, Lacity.org., accessed April 13, 2010.

9. "Basic Color Schemes: Introduction to Color Theory," Tiger Color, accessed August 18, 2011, http://www.tigercolor.com/color-lab/color-theory/color-theory-intro.htm.

10. David A. Livermore, *Cultural Intelligence: Improving Your CQ to Engage Our Multicultural World* (Grand Rapids, Mich.: Baker Academic, 2009), 179.

11. Ibid., 180.

12. Manhattan, New York, has the highest population density of any place in the Western hemisphere with approximately sixty-seven thousand people per square mile or about the same as the most urbanized districts of Hong Kong. Source: "Census 2000 Data for the State of New York," US Census Bureau, accessed on August 18, 2011, http://quickfacts.census.gov/qfd/states/36/3651003.html.

13. United Nations, *World Urbanization Prospects*.

14. Tini Tran, "Pan-Asian Churches Emerging," *Los Angeles Times*, March 8, 1999, http://articles.latimes.com/ 1999/mar/08/news/mn-15199.

15. Ibid.

16. Ibid.

17. These congregations include: Wilshire United Methodist Church, First Church of the Nazarene, Wilshire Christian Church, and First Baptist Church. Source: Keith Watkins, "Multi-Language Congregations: A Field Study in Los Angeles 1993," accessed August 25, 2011, http://www.cts.edu/images/encounter/552kwatkins.pdf?ml=4&mlt=system&tmpl=component (site discontinued).

18. David Britt, "From Homogeneity to Congruence: A Church-Community Model," in *Planting and Growing Urban Churches: From Dream to Reality*, ed. Harvie M. Conn (Grand Rapids, Mich.: Baker, 1997), 138.

19. Ibid.

20. That thought would seem to be supported in Scripture. See Acts 13:1–3.

Chapter 10

1. Mark DeYmaz, *Building a Healthy Multi-Ethnic Church: Mandate, Commitments and Practices of a Diverse Congregation* (San Francisco: Jossey-Bass, 2007), xxvi–xxvii.

2. "Willing to Be Uncomfortable," *EFCA Today* 84, no. 1 (Spring 2010): 11.

3. Mission statement of Reconciliation United Methodist Church, accessed August 14, 2011, http://site.rumcdurham.org.

4. "Willing to Be Uncomfortable."

5. East Liberty Presbyterian Church located in Pittsburg, Pennsylvania, accessed August 1, 2011, http://www.pcusa.org/mulicultural/conteas/winners-slpc.htm (site discontinued).

Chapter 11

1. C. Peter Wagner, "Pathology," *Principles and Procedures of Church Growth* (MN705), Doctor of Ministry Course, Fuller Theological Seminary, February 5–16, 1979, 2.

2. For further research see Gary L. McIntosh, "The Dying Church," in *Taking Your Church to the Next Level: What God You Here Won't Get You There* (Grand Rapids, Mich.: Baker, 2009), 74–86.

3. Arturo Lucero and Robert R. Weaver, "Building Healthy Relationships in a Multi-Ethnic Church with No Ethnic Majority," *Great Commission Research Journal* 2, no. 2 (Winter 2011): 175–195.

4. "Our Vision" Sunrise Church, accessed August 20, 2011, http://www.sunrisechurch.org/vision-rialto.

Chapter 12

1. See Donald A. McGavran, *Understanding Church Growth* (Grand Rapids, Mich.: Eerdmans, 1970); and George G. Hunter III, *To Spread the Power: Church Growth in the Wesleyan Spirit* (Nashville: Abingdon Press, 1987).

2. David A. Livermore, *Cultural Intelligence: Improving Your CQ to Engage Our Multicultural World* (Grand Rapids, Mich.: Baker Academic, 2009), 245–255.

3. See L. R. Hoffman and N. R. F. Maier, "Quality and Acceptance of Problem Solutions by Members of Homogeneous and Heterogeneous Groups," *The Journal of Abnormal and Social Psychology* 62(2), (March 1961): 401–407.

RECOMMENDED READING

Alumkai, Anthony, W. *Asian America Evangelical Churches: Race, Ethnicity, and Assimilation in the Second Generation*. New York: LFB, 2003.

Anderson, David A. *Gracism: The Art of Inclusion*. Downers Grove, Ill.: InterVarsity, 2010.

Anyabwile, Thabiti M. and Mark A. Noll. *The Decline of African-American Theology: From Biblical Faith to Cultural Captivity*. Downers Grove, Ill.: InterVarsity, 2007.

Appleby, Jerry L. *Missions Have Come Home to America: The Church's Cross-Cultural Ministry to Ethnics*. Kansas City, Mo.: Beacon Hill, 1986.

Axtell, Roger E. *Gestures: The Do's and Taboos of Body Language Around the World*. New York: Wiley, 1991.

Bakke, Ray. *A Theology as Big as the City*. Downers Grove, Ill.: InterVarsity, 1997.

Battle, Michael. *The Black Church in America: African American Christian Spirituality*. Malden, Mass.: Blackwell, 2006.

Belew, Wendell. *Missions in the Mosaic*. Atlanta, Ga.: Home Mission Board of the Southern Baptist Convention, 1974.

Berger, Peter L. *The Sacred Canopy: Elements of a Sociological Theory of Religion*. Garden City, N.Y.: Anchor, 1969.

Carle, Robert D. and Louis A. Decaro, Jr., eds. *Signs of Hope in the City: Ministries of Community Renewal*. Valley Forge, Pa.: Judson, 1999.

Carroll R., M. Daniel. *Christians at the Border: Immigration, the Church, and the Bible*. Grand Rapids, Mich.: Baker, 2008.

Carson, D. A. *Christ & Culture Revisited*. Grand Rapids, Mich.: Eerdmans, 2008.

Cavalli-Sforza, L. Luca, Paolo Menozzi, and Alberto. Piazza. *The History and Geography of Human Genes*. Princeton, N.J.: Princeton Press, 1994.

Cha, Peter, S. Steve Kang, and Helen Lee. *Growing Healthy Asian American Churches*. Downers Grove, Ill: InterVarsity, 2006.

Chandler, Paul-Gordon. *God's Global Mosaic: What We Can Learn from Christians Around the World*. Downers Grove, Ill.: InterVarsity, 1997, 2000.

Cone, James H. and Gayraud W. Wilmore. *Black Theology: A Documentary History, Volume II*. Maryknoll, N.Y.: Orbis, 1993.

Conn, Harvie M. *The American City and the Evangelical Church: A Historical Overview*. Grand Rapids, Mich.: Baker, 1994.

————. *A Clarified Vision for Urban Mission: Dispelling the Urban Sterotypes*. Grand Rapids, Mich.: Zondervan, 1987.

————. *Planting and Growing Urban Churches: From Dream to Reality*. Grand Rapids, Mich.: Baker, 1997.

Costen, Melva Wilson. *African American Christian Worship*. Nashville: Abingdon, 1993, 2007.

Crawford, Evans E. *The Hum: Call and Response in African American Preaching*. Nashville: Abingdon, 1995.

Crespo, Orlando. *Being Latino in Christ: Finding Wholeness in Your Ethnic Identity*. Downers Grove, Ill.: InterVarsity, 2003. This book is written for Latinos (the preferred term over Hispanics) but it will offer some insider perspectives on Latinos' concerns and issues for the non-Latino reader.

Davis, James H. and Woodie W. White. *Racial Transition in the Church*. Nashville: Abingdon, 1980.

Dennison, Jack. *City Reaching: On the Road to Community Transformation.* Pasadena, Calif.: William Carey Library, 1999.

DeYmaz, Mark. *Building a Healthy Multi-Ethnic Church: Mandate, Commitments and Practices of a Diverse Congregation.* San Francisco: Jossey-Bass, 2007.

DeYmaz, Mark and Harry Li. *Ethnic Blends: Mixing Diversity into Your Local Church.* Grand Rapids, Mich.: Zondervan, 2010.

Dinnerstein, Leonard, Roger L. Nichols and David M. Reimers. *Natives and Strangers: Ethnic Groups and the Building of America.* New York: Oxford University Press, 1979.

Dodson, Howard, Amiri Baraka, Gail Lumet Buckley, Henry Louis Gates Jr., and Annette Gordon-Reed. *Jubilee: The Emergence of African-American Culture.* Washington, D.C.: National Geographic, 2003.

Driggers, B. Carlisle. *The Church in the Changing Community: Crisis or Opportunity?* Atlanta: Home Mission Board, SBC, 1977.

DuBois, W. E. B. *The Souls of Black Folks.* Seattle: CreateSpace, 2011.

DuBose, Francis M. *How Churches Grow in an Urban World: History, Theology, and Strategy of Growth in All Kinds of City Churches.* Nashville: Broadman, 1978.

Ecklund, Elaine Howard. *Korean American Evangelicals: New Models for Civic Life.* New York: Oxford University Press, 2008.

Fong, Bruce W. *Racial Equality in the Church: A Critique of the Homogeneous Unit Principle in Light of a Practical Theology Perspective.* Lanham, Md.: University Press of America, 1996.

Fussell, Paul. *CLASS: A Guide through the American Status System.* New York: Touchstone, 1992.

Gilmer, Charles. *A Cry of Hope, A Call to Action: Unleashing the Next Generation of Black Christian Leaders.* Lake Mary, Fla.: Creation House, 2009.

Glasser, Arthur F. *Announcing the Kingdom: The Story of God's Mission in the Bible.* Grand Rapids, Mich.: Baker Academic, 2003.

González, Justo L. *Mañana: Christian Theology from a Hispanic Perspective.* Nashville: Abingdon, 1990.

Graves, Joseph L. *The Race Myth: Why We Pretend Race Exists in America.* New York: Plume, 2005.

Grunlan, Stephan A. and Marvin K. Mayers. *Cultural Anthropology: A Christian Perspective.* Grand Rapids, Mich.: Zondervan, 1979.

Hanson, Victor Davis. *Mexifornia: A State of Becoming.* New York: Encounter Books, 2007 (Second Edition).

Harris, Paula and Doug Schaupp. *Being White: Finding Our Place in a Multiethnic World.* Downers Grove, Ill.: InterVarsity, 2004.

Hesselgrave, David. J. *Planting Churches Cross-Culturally: A Guide for Home and Foreign Missions.* Grand Rapids, Mich.: Baker, 1980.

Hiebert, Paul G. *Transforming Worldviews: An Anthropological Understanding of How People Change.* Grand Rapids, Mich.: Baker, 2008.

Hilliard, Jr., Donald. *Church Growth from an African American Perspective.* Valley Forge, Pa.: Judson, 2006.

Hinton, Keith. *Growing Churches Singapore Style: Ministry in an Urban Context.* Republic of Singapore: Overseas Missionary Fellowship, 1985.

Horton, James Oliver and Lois E. *A History of the African American People: The History, Traditions & Culture of African Americans.* Detroit, Mich.: Wayne State University Press, 1997.

Lingenfelter, Sherwood. *Leading Cross-Culturally: Covenant Relationships for Effective Christian Leadership.* Grand Rapids, Mich.: Baker Books, 2008.

———. *Transforming Culture: A Challenge for Christian Mission.* Grand Rapids, Mich.: Baker, 1992.

Lingenfelter, Sherwood G. and Marvin K. Mayers. *Ministering Cross-Culturally*: An Incarnational Model for Personal Relationships. Grand Rapids, Mich.: Baker, 1986, 2002.

Linthicum, Robert C. *City of God, City of Satan: A Biblical Theology of the Urban Church.* Grand Rapids, Mich.: Zondervan, 1991.

Livermore, David A. *Cultural Intelligence: Improving Your CQ to Engage Our Multicultural World.* Grand Rapids, Mich.: Baker Academic, 2009.

Maynard-Reid, Pedrito U. *Diverse Worship: African-American, Caribbean & Hispanic Perspectives.* Downers Grove, Ill.: InterVarsity, 2000.

McGavran, Donald A. *Ethnic Realties and the Church: Lessons from India.* South Pasadena, Calif.: William Carey Library, 1979.

———. *Understanding Church Growth.* Grand Rapids, Mich.: Eerdmans, 1970.

Milne, Bruce. *Dynamic Diversity: Bridging Class, Age, Race and Gender in the Church.* Downers Grove, Ill.: InterVarsity Academic, 2007.

Montoya, Alex D. *Hispanic Ministry in North America.* Grand Rapids, Mich.: Ministry Resources Library, 1987.

Nida, Eugene A. *Customs & Cultures: Anthropology for Christian Missions.* New York: Harper & Row, 1954.

———. *Understanding Latin America.* Pasadena, Cal.: William Carey Library, 1974.

Ortiz, Manual. *The Hispanic Challenge: Opportunities Confronting the Church.* Downers Grove, Ill.: InterVarsity, 1993.

———. *One New People: Models for Developing a Multiethnic Church.* Downers Grove, Ill.: InterVarsity, 1996.

Pinn, Anthony and Benjamin Valentin. *Creating Ourselves: African Americans and Hispanic Americans of Popular Culture and Religious Expression.* Durham, N.C.: Duke University Press, 2009.

Rah, Soong-Chan. *Many Colors: Cultural Intelligence for a Changing Church.* Chicago: Moody, 2010.

———. *The Next Evangelicalism: Freeing the Church from Western Cultural Captivity.* Downers Grove, Ill.: InterVarsity, 2009.

Robinson, John D. and Larry C. James. *Diversity in Human Interaction: The Tapestry of America.* New York: Oxford University Press, 2003.

Roll, Samuel and Mark Irwin. *The Invisible Border: Latinos in America.* Boston: Intercultural Press, 2008.

Rose, Jerry D. *Peoples: The Ethnic Dimension in Human Relations.* Chicago: Rand McNally College, 1976.

Rose, Larry L. and C. Kirk Hadaway, eds. *The Urban Challenge: Reaching America's Cities with the Gospel.* Nashville: Broadman, 1982.

———. *An Urban World: Churches Face the Future.* Nashville: Broadman, 1984.

Sanchez, Daniel R. and Rudolph D. Gonzalez. *Sharing the Good News with Our Roman Catholic Friends.* Atlanta: Church Starting Network, 2003.

Sanders, Cheryl J. *Saints in Exile: The Holiness Pentecostal Experience in the African American Religion and Culture.* New York: Oxford University Press, 1999.

Schlermerhorn, R. A. *Comparative Ethnic Relations: A Framework for Theory and Research.* Chicago: University of Chicago Press, 1979.

Smith, Efrem and Phil Jackson. *The Hip-Hop Church: Connecting with the Movement Shaping Our Culture.* Downers Grove, Ill.: InterVarsity, 2005.

Sowell, Thomas. *Race and Culture: A World View.* New York: BasicBooks, 1994.

Van Engen, Charles. *God's Missionary People: Rethinking the Purpose of the Local Church.* Grand Rapids, Mich.: Baker, 1991.

————. *Mission on the Way: Issues in Mission Theology.* Grand Rapids. Mich.: Baker, 1996.

Wagner, C. Peter. *Our Kind of People: The Ethical Dimensions of Church Growth in America.* Atlanta: John Knox, 1979.

Woodley, Randy. *Living in Color: Embracing God's Passion for Ethnic Diversity.* Downers Grove, Ill.: InterVarsity, 2001.

ABOUT THE AUTHORS AND SERVICES AVAILABLE

Gary L. McIntosh, DMin, PhD, is an internationally known author, speaker, consultant, and professor of Christian ministry and leadership at Talbot School of Theology, Biola University, located in La Mirada, California. He has written extensively in the field of pastoral ministry, leadership, generational studies, and church growth.

Dr. McIntosh received his BA from Colorado Christian University in biblical studies, an MDiv from Western Seminary in pastoral studies, a DMin from Fuller Theological Seminary in church growth studies, and a PhD from Fuller Theological Seminary in intercultural studies.

As president of the Church Growth Network, a church consulting firm he founded in 1989, Dr. McIntosh has served over five thousand churches in eighty-three denominations throughout the United States and Canada. The 1995 and 1996 president of the American Society for Church Growth, he edited the *Journal of the American Society for Church Growth* for fourteen years. He currently edits *Growth Points*, a nationally read newsletter offering insights for ministry leaders in the United States and Canada. Gary and his wife of forty-four years, Carol, have two grown sons and six grandchildren.

Alan McMahan, PhD, has served in churches in North America and on the Pacific Rim as well as taught in the areas of missiology, church growth, leadership, organizational development, and evangelism. He is active in training undergraduate and graduate students including mid-career professionals, Bible school teachers, pastors, and denominational leaders throughout the United States, Canada, and much of Southeast Asia in the effective means to develop leaders and grow churches.

Dr. McMahan maintains an active consulting service for churches and is a former president of the American Society of Church Growth. He has earned degrees from Fuller Seminary, Asbury Seminary, the Alliance Theological Seminary, and Nyack College. His PhD dissertation was entitled "Training Turnaround Leaders, Systemic Approaches to Reinstate Growth in Plateaued Churches." He has served as vice president for the Alliance Theological Seminary, and as the academic dean at The King's College in mid-town Manhattan. Dr. McMahan now works at Biola University as an associate professor in the School of Intercultural Studies and serves as the department chair for the undergraduate program. He has a wife, Terri, and two sons, Billy and Jonathan, and lives in La Mirada, California.

SERVICES AVAILABLE

Gary L. McIntosh and Alan McMahan speak to numerous churches, nonprofit organizations, schools, and conventions each year. Services available include keynote presentations at major meetings, seminars and workshops, training courses, courses at colleges and universities, and ongoing consultation.

For a live presentation of the material found in *Being the Church in a Multi-Ethnic Community* or to request a catalog of materials or other information on Gary's or Alan's availability and ministry, contact:

Gary L. McIntosh, PhD
Church Growth Network
PO Box 892589
Temecula, CA 92589-2589
951-506-3086

Alan McMahan, PhD
Biola University
13800 Biola Ave.
La Mirada, CA 90639
562-903-6000

www.ChurchGrowthNetwork.com

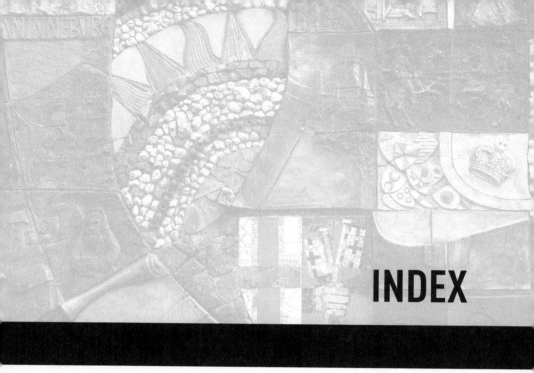

INDEX

Unleash Your Church!

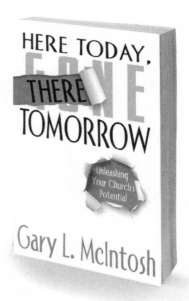

Church leaders are frustrated! Larger churches are bogged down by the weight of their own organizations, and smaller churches struggle with the inability to get things moving. Veteran leadership expert Gary L. McIntosh provides help to leaders of churches, regardless of size, who struggle to create workable plans to move their congregation forward. This book identifies the best practices on how to assess the unique identity of a church and design a plan for its future.

Here Today, There Tomorrow
Unleashing Your Church's Potential
Gary L. McIntosh

Price: $14.99
ISBN: 978-0-89827-422-6

For more information go to
www.wesleyan.org/catalog.

wesleyan
publishing
house

www.wesleyan.org/wph
1.800.493.7539

Embrace the World at Your Door!

With his conversational style and humorous anecdotes, Jim Lo will show how your church can open up to those in your community from different countries and cultures.

Intentional Diversity
Creating Cross-Cultural Ministry Relationships in Your Church
Jim Lo
Price: $7.99
ISBN: 978-0-89827-242-0